HOW TO BUILD
WINNING
TEAMS
AGAIN AND AGAIN...

and Have People Asking How You Did It

JAMES SCOULLER

Dedication

This book is dedicated to Oliver Alan Scouller,
my five-year-old grandson, and every
child of his generation in every country.

HAWKHURST
Publishing

First paperback edition published in 2024 in the United Kingdom
by Hawkhurst Publishing, Bedford

Tel: +44 (0)1525 718023
Website: **www.leadershipmasterysuite.com**

Interior book design by Silke Spingies

ISBN 978 1 7392766 0 7 (paperback)
ISBN 978 1 7392766 1 4 (ebook)

Contents

Preface to Book One   7

1 This Pathway & Its Payoffs   11

2 A Work Group In Turmoil   23

3 It Takes Effort to Create Teams   29

4 The Team Progression Curve   51

5 Performance Groups and Real Teams   69

6 Why So Few Senior Teams?   83

7 Seeing Through the Fog I:
   Commit-Combust-Combine (Overview)   95

8 Seeing Through the Fog II:
   Commit-Combust-Combine (Detail)   119

9 Seeing Through the Fog III:
   Evolution and Endings   161

10 The Next Step   169

Appendix The Hidden Psychology of Teams   173

Notes   203

Bibliography   217

Index   221

About the Author   225

Preface to Book One

Why I've Written This

In my view – and in my experience – we pay too little attention to helping people learn the art of team building and regeneration. Ask yourself, do companies spend much time and money on the subject? No. Do business schools offer deep dives into the challenge of building successful teams again and again? No. Yet much of a company's success depends on its people's ability to collaborate. The same is true of every country's economy. Don't you find this odd?

I do. And the older I get the stranger it seems. That's why I've written this trilogy. I want to help individuals, their teams and their companies master the art of team building.

I won't pretend; it hasn't been a straightforward project. From beginning to end it's taken seventeen years. If you'd told me in 2007, when I started, that this material won't appear before 2024, I'd have felt discouraged. But therein lay my naivety. The truth is, it's taken this long to disperse the fog and discern the few principles that really matter … and then test them in the marketplace with my coaching clients.

Gaining experience on what works and what doesn't was crucial – crucial for my confidence and for making sure I don't waste your time in reading this trilogy. My task was to simplify what I was learning so you can grasp it, but not oversimplify to the point where you miss important subtleties.

Why A Trilogy?

I was asked during the writing, "Why a trilogy, why not one book?" My original aim was to write just the one book. But though readers of my previous work, The Three Levels of Leadership, know how much I dislike padded writing, my preference for succinctness didn't stop the manuscript expanding beyond my original vision.

While writing what is now the third book, I consulted publishing experts who told me something I didn't know: that in the last ten years, on average, nonfiction books have halved in length. It's clear that readers prefer shorter more manageable nonfiction. One remarked, "If you need that material, and I believe you do, and if the book has distinct sections, why not make it a series?"

I'd already designed the book to have three parts – what you need to *know*, what you need to *do* and *how* to do it – so it wasn't a difficult decision. A trilogy was born.

Chapter Numbering

While you won't notice anything unusual in this first volume, I've chosen to treat the chapter numbering as though the trilogy is one book. So when you get to Book Two you'll find it starts at chapter 11. For the same reason, Book Three starts at chapter 22. I have two aims in adopting this unorthodox approach. First, to remind readers that there's a definite thread running through all three books – that although they're distinct, they're connected, they build on one another. Second, to make referencing of previous chapters in my earlier books easier – I felt it might be less confusing to readers if each chapter was uniquely numbered.

Relationship To My First Book

The Three Levels of Leadership, my first book, came out in 2011. I released an expanded second edition in 2016.

"Three Levels" was – and remains – a self-help manual for leaders. It had one gap in its content: it said nothing about group psychology and team building. As I remarked in that book, leaders need to understand the psychology of small and large groups and how to intercept their hidden forces if they're to build cohesive teams and companies. However, I knew any effort to plug the hole would make the book unwieldy. That's why I wrote in chapter 7, "I plan to follow The Three Levels of Leadership in 2017 with a practical book on teams and their psychology to give you a companion learning source."

I missed that deadline by seven years but this trilogy is that companion source. "Three Levels" and "Winning Teams" therefore have a sibling relationship.

Website

If you're aiming for maximum benefit from the ideas and advice in this Winning Teams series you'll want to know about the free stuff on offer at my Leadership Mastery Suite website. Here's its address:

www.leadershipmasterysuite.com

There you can sign up to gain free access to all my articles and videos on leadership and team building or to download copies of my tools. The tools come from this Winning Teams series *and* The Three Levels of Leadership. You'll also be first to hear about any free webinars.

Acknowledgements

I couldn't have written these books without spending 28 years in industry and another 19 years as an executive coach. For me, ideas are important, but they must be forged and refined in the workspace. So my thanks go to former colleagues and clients.

Special thanks too to the small bank of beta readers who kindly agreed to review all three manuscripts and give me their candid feedback. I can assure you they did. They are Jim Kennedy, John Webster, Jacki Evans, Mark Renshaw, Chris Smith and Professor Jerry Estenson. The trilogy is better for their input.

Graham Lee, a fellow author, coach and unofficial beta reader also gave valuable advice, especially on seven chapters. Thank you Graham.

Finally, there's my wife, Trish. It isn't easy being married to someone who sets out on a years-long project that becomes an obsession. And yet she's coped throughout, never expressing doubts about the value of what I've been trying to write. How do you thank the woman you love, your life partner for over 40 years, in words that do her justice? I really don't know. But to you Trish, once again, my love and thanks.

James Scouller
Flitwick, Bedfordshire
June 2023

1

This Pathway & Its Payoffs

Welcome to the first book in the How To Build Winning Teams Again and Again trilogy, the series of handbooks for people who are serious about leading, building and regenerating great teams.

In this, Book One, I explain what you need to *know* about the psychological challenges of creating teams. Book Two outlines what you need to *do* to build them and Book Three shows *how* to apply Book Two's principles in different scenarios.

Together, the three books offer a pathway to success in one of the most difficult challenges in organisational life: building successful teams – not just once, but repeatedly.

The Payoffs

What will you gain from reading this and the next two books in the trilogy? Well, think of a few outstanding companies. Ask yourself, "Why are they exceptional?" Perhaps you said it's because they're great at creating new products and services, disrupting old industries with a new business model, executing strategy, improving or delivering fabulous customer service, growing sales or cutting lead times. Whatever your answer, here's the common thread: beyond the startup stage their results didn't come from individuals working solo. They relied on people working together across disciplines to mesh their multiple skills and experiences.

Those companies prove that delivering superb results while standing out from competitors relies on combining human talents. And teams are the key to that – they are the building blocks to companywide collaboration. Indeed, you could relabel "team building" as "the art of human collaboration". Simply put, your ability to build and nurture teams determines whether you achieve consistent high performance across your department or business.

So what will you gain from reading this trilogy? Well, it depends on your role. If you lead or work in teams it'll show you how to not only improve their results, but also how to make working together a more fulfilling experience. If you're a CEO it'll help you raise the top team's game, meaning you model the way for everyone else in your business. And if you're the Chief People Officer it'll give you the chance to build the ultimate competitive advantage in the 21st century: scalable skill in the art of human collaboration.

A Competitive Advantage?

Wait, what? A competitive advantage? Really? Yes, in my view a genuine lasting advantage.

Think about it: what makes something a true competitive advantage? Sure, the company's products or services must have a strong "plus" that customers prefer down the years, whether it's based on branding, low cost, a patent, superior design, a unique production method or perhaps the way employees interact with customers. But whatever it is, *it must be difficult for competitors to copy*. If it's not hard to duplicate it won't be a lasting advantage. And in my experience, if you can bake a companywide ability to build winning teams again and again across the board into your culture, your rivals will find it incredibly hard to copy.

Team Building Isn't Easy

Why will it be so difficult to copy? Partly because it takes time to build any culture-based advantage but mainly because mastering the art of team building isn't easy. It's the flipside of the reason why becoming great at team building in every part of your business can give you such a lasting advantage.

Yet down the years I've heard people say about team building, "It's not rocket science." These days, having worked in teams, led teams, and coached teams for forty-five years, my stock response is, "No it's not, it's harder than rocket science." Talk to rocket scientists and in essence they'll tell you, "It's not complicated. You need to meet three challenges: get the rocket moving, overcome the pull of gravity and plot a course ... and all three depend on Isaac Newton's laws of motion and physical gravitation." In other words, you can use equations from physics to predict and control what will happen.[1]

That's not true of teams. Teams are made up of human beings. We have free will, meaning we can change our minds at any time, making unpredictability a constant factor. And as I'll explain in chapter 3, you'll also see an array of subterranean psychological forces in teams that collide, confusing the members and making it harder to achieve success. My point is that building winning teams that last – and rebuilding them when they break up as they always do – is a demanding, complex challenge.

I often compare it to solving a Rubik's Cube puzzle. Older readers will remember the Rubik's Cube craze in the 1980s but younger people may not know it. It was a three-dimensional puzzle. Like all cubes it had six faces. But as the illustration shows, the Rubik's Cube comprised 27 smaller coloured cubes arranged in a 3x3x3 grid. When  you first unwrapped it, the mini cubes making up each face showed the same colour. However, because you could twist and rotate every column and row, within a few random moves you could scramble the colours to produce a patchwork quilt arrangement. Your aim was to figure out how to rotate and twist the Rubik's Cube to restore one uniform colour to each face. If you knew what you were doing, you could restore any messy combination within twenty moves. The difficulty? In scrambling the colours you inadvertently created one of trillions of possible combinations, so returning to your starting point was tricky. But now imagine a Rubik's Cube where not only can you move every row and column, the mini cubes' colours also keep changing every hour. Successful long-term team building and renewal is similarly complex and challenging.

Look at how many of the great – and I mean great – professional football club coaches and managers are sacked every year. Few leave their jobs voluntarily. Even fewer have shown they can build and rebuild teams over five years or more. Perhaps Sir Alex Ferguson and Pep Guardiola are exceptions, but that's the point, they're exceptions.[2] Why are they exceptions? Because team building is a difficult art.

That's why so many work teams run into trouble. In a 2015 Harvard Business Review article, having studied 95 teams in 25 leading companies, all chosen by an independent panel of academics and experts, Behnam Tabrizi reported that 75% of cross-functional teams fail. Not only did he find that three-quarters of them were dysfunctional, they also failed on at least three of five criteria: (1) meeting budget; (2) staying on schedule; (3) adhering to specifications; (4) meeting customer expectations; (5) staying aligned with the company's goals.[3] His isn't an isolated study – others have reported similarly dismal findings.[4]

This data shows how difficult companies find it to build winning teams once, never mind repeatedly. And it's precisely because it is hard to create winning teams that becoming good at team building again and again across your company can be a source of lasting competitive advantage. If you can do it well, consistently, you can expect remarkable results.

Being Ready To Learn

Because it's difficult, it takes a little time and effort to learn how to build and rebuild winning teams. Yet I know from experience how tough it is for hard-pressed time-poor executives to accept this message. Typically, they'll say something like, "James, I don't have time for all this, can't you just cut to the chase and tell me the key to building winning teams?" Believe me, I would if I could. But listen to the top football coaches when journalists ask them, "What's the key to great team performance / winning the championship / turning your results around?" They often answer something like, "The key is that there's no single key."

In the Frequently Asked Questions chapter towards the end of Book

Three, you'll find a question reflecting this "tell me the quick-and-easy answer" mindset. It goes like this: "What are the three most important ingredients to creating successful teams?" I didn't duck the question. I explained the complexity around team building but because he insisted on three suggestions, I gave him just that. But I added that they wouldn't head off all the would-be team's inevitable challenges or guarantee they'd become a successful team. Also, simply knowing the three headline actions wasn't enough because he needed to grasp the detailed knowhow underlying each one.

The reality is this: if you want to master the art of building winning teams again and again there are things to study, grasp and practise. It will pay off big time, but you need to put the time in.

Ask yourself, how much time have you and your colleagues spent on *consciously* studying, learning and practising how to build teams? Two months? Two weeks? Two days? One day? Less?

When I've put this question to clients down the years they've looked sheepish and admitted that – at best – they may have gone on a two-day bonding exercise in the woods or attended a one-day workshop. Most haven't had any formal training or coaching on the subject. Yet consider how long doctors have to train for – it's typically about seven years. Lawyers? Six years. Architects? Seven years. Accountants? Four years. Why do we expect professionals like these to put years into learning their craft while so many of us think we can take on the difficult art of team building with no prior learning?

Would you let someone operate on your body following a one-day workshop on human anatomy? Would you and your family drive across a one-thousand-foot-high bridge built by an architect whose only learning came from a 48-hour awayday event? Would you trust your financial controller if he or she had no training in accountancy? Would you let a lawyer represent you in a life-or-death case in court after attending only a three-day "Essentials of Criminal Law" workshop? Of course you wouldn't. So why have we adopted such a casual attitude to the difficult art of building successful teams when it can make such a huge difference to results?

I therefore suggest you pause and examine your mindset around team building and your readiness to learn. Are you hoping that within a few short pages you'll have grasped the keys to creating winning teams, meaning you can make a name for yourself in whatever way motivates you? If that's you, I must point out that you may find this trilogy a frustrating read in the early stages. Why? Because it starts with the fundamentals, meaning you won't have the how-to answers immediately. But you will find that as we get to the action-related stuff in books 2 and 3, you'll have acquired the grounding to start putting the ideas into action. If you jump straight to the action principles in book 2 and the how-to-apply-them road maps in book 3, you will lack the ideas and models to build on them. In other words, you'll be building on sand.

If there is one key you're looking for, it is to practise what in Zen they call "beginner's mind" as you start reading these books. This won't be straightforward for more experienced executives but it's nevertheless important. Beginner's mind is free of fixed expectations, prejudgements and mindsets and accepts there's always more to learn. It's the mind that's not already made up, that's comfortable with saying "I don't know" and letting go of previous beliefs, replacing them with a better understanding. I'm not saying you shouldn't appreciate your existing expertise and experience. But I am suggesting that on this high-payoff but understudied subject of team building you consciously make yourself ready to learn the fundamentals before getting on to the applied stuff. That way, not only will you learn, I think you'll enjoy the experience of reading these books, starting with the one in your hands.

In short, think of this as a course in team building where we start with the basics. However, don't be fooled. They may be the "basics" but I can assure you most readers won't be familiar with them. Indeed many – perhaps you included – are in for some surprises.

The Evidence

How do you know this stuff will work? Or will work for you? If you're talking about intellectual certainty, the short answer is that you won't know for sure. But as you read the content your intuition will tell you if you're tapping into something that will help you, your team, your department or your company. Listen to that voice within that says, "Yes, this feels true, this feels right, this makes sense."

However, to feed the more rational side of your mind, I'll give you some data and then a story. To start, here are before-and-after profiles for two senior teams I coached in different industries, one in 2007 and the other in 2011, using the ideas, principles and tools you'll find in this trilogy. Indeed, it was through these and similar experiences that I had the chance to test and refine them down the years.

Team Ratings on 25 Key Attributes & Behaviours

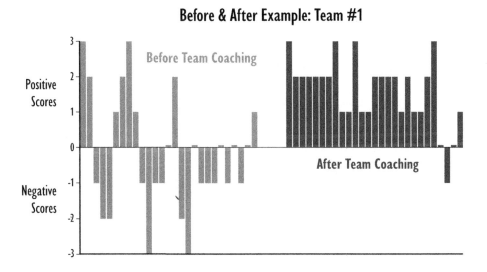

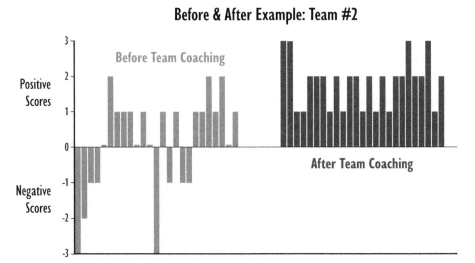

Each bar represents a team quality (for example, skills and knowhow) or behaviour (for example, saying what they really think and feel). Scores above the horizontal line are strengths while those below are weaknesses. Can you see the differences between the light bars (before coaching) and dark bars (after coaching)? They show the huge shift in both profiles. Both teams upped their game rapidly. They removed their greatest weaknesses while boosting their strengths. People outside the two teams confirmed that they'd changed. More important, both teams delivered results they'd struggled to achieve before.

Here's a third more recent example involving another leadership team but using an updated rating system like the one I describe in chapter 27 (Book Three):

Team Ratings on 70 Key Attributes & Behaviours

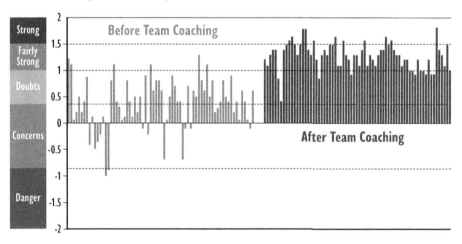

Once again, you can see advances in the team's ability to deliver under pressure. The team felt it. Others in the organisation noticed it. Not surprisingly, their results improved.

I must stress that the process of building and improving teams is not like baking a chocolate dump cake. You don't just assemble the ingredients, follow a recipe faithfully and then "bam", there's your guaranteed result. It's definitely an art not a science. In the third example they worked with me as a team coach for over six months and I recall making mistakes and overlooking signs of problems we could have addressed earlier. Although they improved hugely, they still had weaknesses when we ended (you can see some of their post-coaching scores were in the "Doubts" zone), which is why they didn't regard themselves as a fully-fledged team at that point. Nevertheless, by using the ideas you'll find in this book, applying the seven action principles in Book 2, and following one of the road maps you'll read about in Book 3, this team made notable progress with me and continued to climb what I call the Team Progression Curve (you'll read about it in chapter 4) without me.

Now the story:

> The newly-hired European president of a $500 million company was worried. His business was growing market share and its margins were good, but he felt they wouldn't hit their long-term target of being #2 in Europe without shifting direction. He was wondering: "Am I right? And, if so, what are we going to do?"
>
> He found himself hesitating for two reasons. First, he suspected that any change of strategy would be controversial. Why? Because it would demand a new vision, a new agenda, and mean committing to fresh initiatives while switching off old projects to create capacity for action. Second, he'd inherited a group of independently-minded colleagues who largely worked apart and wouldn't take kindly to someone telling them to change direction.
>
> He decided not to impose his views. Instead, he brought me in to guide him and his nine colleagues through a team coaching process with three aims:
>
> - See whether others also felt they would miss their chief aim of being #2 in Europe.
> - Decide what, together, they were going to do about it.
> - Ensure that whatever they agreed turned into concrete action, which meant becoming a real team.
>
> We embarked on an eleven-day three-phase programme over seven months. Woven into the coaching were exercises to create a stronger sense of togetherness, openness and trust. Why? So that when they worked on the intellectual content, they said what they were really thinking and feeling and genuinely committed themselves to following through.

Phase #1 took 2 days. It focused on turning their "Reach number two in our industry" aim into a firm sales target and then producing a shared forecast to see what size of gap they were facing. They were shocked. They found that – even if all of their new products and geographical expansions succeeded – they'd miss their target of being #2 by 5% points of market share (or $140 million in sales). Sure, they'd grow faster than the market, but they'd miss their chief ambition by a mile. What did they see as their biggest single issue once they'd learned this? That they lacked a compelling vision.

Creating this vision became the aim of phase #2, which took place over 2 days. Having examined their shared values, competencies, ideas, customers' aspirations and competitors' weaknesses they carved out a simple but remarkable vision. A vision that excited them. A vision they wanted to be part of. A vision they believed could plug the $140 million gap.

Phase #3 took place in three parts over 7 days. We focused on action alternatives, assessment of options, action choices and commitment to actions. Not surprisingly, it produced heated debate.

The result? They achieved the all-important dissatisfaction with the status quo needed to shift them into a higher gear. They created a distinctive vision giving them a real chance of achieving the #2 position in Europe. And they agreed a programme that united them and gained their European subsidiary MDs' backing. The HR director, who'd been present over the 11 days, wrote afterwards to say, "*Terrific… an energised team who want to make a difference.*" Three years later – two years ahead of target – they became #2 in Europe. As I write this eleven years on, they are now #1.

The Pathway

Earlier I posed an unanswered question: why have we adopted such a casual attitude to the difficult art of building successful teams when it can make such a huge difference to results? In my view, it's because until now we've had no widely understood theory explaining teams' hidden psychological blocks nor a convincing action model for addressing them.

This trilogy of handbooks is designed to change that. For the first time, it offers you the chance to grasp the psychology, principles and road maps to team success.

This instalment, Book One, concentrates on the psychology and other essential basics – the stuff you need to *know*. You'll learn:

- The hidden traps facing your group and why it takes effort to create teams.
- About the Team Progression Curve.
- Why you need to grasp the contrast between performance groups and real teams.
- Why so few senior management groups have become genuine teams (until now).
- The three psychological challenges your team faces in climbing the curve.
- How to recognise which of the three challenges – Commit, Combust or Combine (C-C-C) – are affecting your team most.

When you've finished this book you've set yourself up for Book Two – the "what you need to *do*" book. It'll offer a seven-principle (7P) action model for nailing the issues you'll read about here and give practical tips you can quickly apply.

You could stop after Book Two if you just want to understand teams' hidden psychological forces – the stuff stopping them succeeding – and grasp intellectually what you (or perhaps others in your company) should do about them.

However, if you want to go beyond mere intellectual understanding and apply the second book successfully, Book Three is its "*how* to" companion.

It will show you how to diagnose what's happening in your team using a tool I call TeamFixer®, figure out which of the seven principles to concentrate on and how to sequence your actions to best effect in three scenarios: a new team, an existing team that's doing okay but could do better, and a team with serious problems. It also offers you an FAQs chapter. There I've answered 40 practical questions asked by people like you, people I've worked with over the last nineteen years as their coach. Finally, if you're a coach, it'll explain how to apply the C-C-C and 7P models in your work with clients.

Thus, you could summarise the pathway you'll be following as Theory – Practical – Applied.

One final point: you don't need a coach to apply what you'll read in this trilogy. My aim in writing is to teach you and your colleagues how to build, uphold and restore teams by yourselves. That doesn't mean you shouldn't consider hiring a coach because, being a specialist, he or she should be able to quicken your progress, but it's not a must.

Now let's get into the content, starting with a short story of a real-life work group struggling to deliver...

2

A Work Group In Turmoil

It's the morning of 10 December 2020. Christmas is coming and Britain, like every other country, is in the grip of the Covid 19 pandemic.

In Handforth, Cheshire, 10 miles south of Manchester, six parish council members are bracing themselves for that evening's extraordinary session, a meeting that'll become world-famous. Antivirus-spreading rules mean they can't meet face-to-face so they'll be using Zoom video.

The Build-Up

The build-up to the meeting has been stormy...

It all started six years earlier. New council members had fresh ideas. They proposed a council Facebook page, an after-school club and policies to guide house building on precious green belt land. But other members opposed their plans. They blocked the projects. Meetings became testy. Councillors started hurling "conflict of interest" accusations. Their opponents would read lawyers' statements aloud. It was hard to get anything done.

Handforth residents started complaining at public meetings. They couldn't understand why their representatives weren't working together to do their best for the town. One said, "*I've attended many council meetings and seen members behave badly. You're there to represent us and do the best for us; you shouldn't bring personal issues into these meetings.*" Another commented, "*The councillors need to improve their teamwork and stop behaving like*

Westminster." A newspaper described the council meetings as "*full of petty arguments about points of order and whether they'd agreed agenda items*". It claimed there was minimal real content.

But nothing changed. Frustration and resentment continued to build. Residents began protesting in writing to Cheshire East Council, which governs the region covering Handforth. In July 2020, five months before the fateful meeting, officials at Cheshire East became so anxious they launched an investigation.

The head of Governance & Compliance for Cheshire East wrote a stern letter to Handforth's council members. I'm paraphrasing but in effect he said: "I've received complaints about how you're running Handforth's affairs and how some of you are behaving. It's alleged that certain council decisions resulting in financial outlays were unlawful so I've started an investigation. My conclusions could result in legal proceedings." Things were getting serious.

The tension rose another notch in November, five weeks before the meeting. One councillor had been skipping meetings for 12 months. According to the rules, that disqualified him. Cheshire East told the parish council clerk that Handforth needed a new ward election to fill the vacancy. The clerk – a full-time employee, effectively the CEO – passed on the news to his council members. Outraged, the chair and two allies insisted he reinstate their colleague. Guided by law, he refused. So they conspired to remove him. Unfortunately, while plotting, one of their emails went astray, landing in the clerk's inbox. Basically it said "*...How can we remove [clerk]? Can we get a solicitor specialising in employment law to get rid of him?*" Despite nearly botching their coup, the chair and his two colleagues managed to suspend the clerk. But by throwing petrol on to burning embers they'd started a blaze they couldn't control. It tore the council in two.

Two of the other Handforth councillors had had enough. They decided to rebel. They sought an extraordinary meeting but the council chair said "no". By following legal procedure, the two rebels insisted and prevailed. The meeting was set for 10 December.

The Meeting

It's approaching 7 PM on the 10th. The councillors and eleven members of the public are settling into their chairs for their soon-to-be unforgettable meeting. Or rather two meetings on separate subjects, one following the other. But this event is different from previous sessions: it has a powerful guest attendee, Jackie Weaver. Ms Weaver leads a Cheshire body that helps local councils perform their duties. She's been parachuted in to improve conduct of Handforth's turbulent meetings.

The first meeting starts with the chair wrongly declaring it illegal. Arguments erupt. They end swiftly when Ms Weaver kicks out three rowdy councillors, including the chair, placing them in the Zoom waiting room. With them gone the others complete the first agenda in 30 minutes.

The second meeting begins chaotically straight afterwards with the three ejected councillors back in the virtual meeting room and members of the public watching on. One councillor asks, *"When are we starting?"* Another quietly mutters in a threatening voice, *"F**k off!"* It's open warfare.

The chair – who inexplicably is calling himself the clerk – once again declares the meeting invalid as, he argues, it hasn't followed the law. When Jackie Weaver points out, correctly, that this isn't true, the chair bellows *"Will you stop talking..."*. Ms Weaver responds, *"If you keep disrupting the meeting, I'll have to remove you."* *"You can't,"* yell the chair's two supporters. The chair adds, *"Only the chair can remove people from the meeting."* Raising his voice he growls, *"You have no authority here, Jackie Weaver, no authority at all!"* He's wrong. He finds himself back in the Zoom waiting room. His two allies are livid.

Ms Weaver invites the remaining members to elect a new chair for the meeting. The vice-chair, one of the two allies, thunders, *"They can't, I'm vice-chair, I take charge."* His voice quivering with rage, he roars, *"Read the standing orders, read them and understand them!"* Other council members gasp in horror at his ferocity. Before he can say anything else, Jackie Weaver slings him out and he joins his friend in the waiting room. She repeats her invitation to elect a new chair for the meeting. The remaining ally protests, declaring *"You don't know what you're talking about"*. Ms Weaver groans,

"*We've been through this already, councillor.*" He continues arguing so he too is thrown out. At this point, the meeting explodes into semi-hysterical mirth. One councillor complains that another attendee is behaving like a "*laughing hyena*".

The three allies, locked in the Zoom waiting room, try holding an impromptu secret conversation. They switch to different software. Unfortunately, their pal, perched on a sofa while viewing the videoed council meeting, accidentally reveals this to everyone watching. "*We're trying to have a (Microsoft) Teams meeting you fool,*" hisses his furious (ejected) councillor friend who's sharing his lounge. This triggers further hilarity.

Jackie Weaver asks the remaining councillors if they want her to bring back the noisy trio, but they vote "no".

The meeting calms down, the members elect a stand-in chair for the meeting, and they work through the agenda.

The Aftermath

The meeting's over but deep divisions remain. The rival groups continue trading punches into the new year.

It's the afternoon of 4 February 2021. Suddenly, the painful warring fizzles out. Why? For a reason no one in Handforth could have predicted: the digital equivalent of a meteor strike.

On Twitter, a teenager posts a YouTube video of the council's verbal brawl two months earlier. It goes viral. Six million people around the globe tune in to watch, fascinated. Handforth council achieves instant notoriety. To her astonishment, Jackie Weaver wins overnight fame for her calmness under fire and appears on British television shows.

As winter fades into spring and spring gives way to summer, one by one, the three allies, embarrassed by the episode, resign their council roles. Voters elect three new councillors. The six council members reinstate the clerk, choose a new permanent chair and get down to work.

Seven years have passed.[5]

The Questions

Why did the council members struggle to get things done and endure pain for so long? And indeed why do so many work groups experience crippling obstacles? That's what we'll uncover in the next chapter.

3

It Takes Effort to Create Teams

Chapter two told the story of Handforth Council's seven-year ordeal. Why recount its painful experience? Because it sets up this chapter's big message:

> *It takes conscious effort to build teams to succeed and keep on succeeding, partly because their members must apply disciplines many of them find uncomfortable, but mainly because they face powerful, hidden, unhelpful psychological forces few people know about. To be blunt, if you don't attend to those forces, don't expect your group to become a team and perform like winners.*

When I say, "it takes conscious effort to build teams", I'm talking specifically about teams, not work groups in general. You'll see three basic types of groups in the workplace: task groups, performance groups and real teams. If you imagine a "results scale", task groups sit at the bottom, performance groups in the middle and real teams at the top. Teams are the most ambitious, creative form of work group you'll find. I'll give greater detail on the contrasts between the work groups in chapter 4, but here's my definition of a real team:

> A small group of people with complementary skills and roles who commit to a specific challenging common purpose, blend their abilities and hold one another accountable for delivering collective work outputs and results.

The Handforth councillors weren't aiming to act as a team. They weren't chosen for their complementary skills, they had no agreed specific challenging purpose and certainly weren't holding one another accountable until the two rebels said "enough" after seven years. Instead they were trying to work as a simple task group, the least go-getting, least demanding form of work group. Yet they experienced years of turmoil. And there's my point: even the simplest form of work group can hit bumps in the road. But when the stakes rise – as they do in teams – their obstacles multiply. If you've worked in teams or watched them in action you'll know most don't perform to their highest potential. Indeed, as I pointed out in chapter 1, recent research shows that 75% of teams fail.[6]

The question is, why do adults find it so difficult to work successfully in teams?

It's because real teams don't form effortlessly. Yes, theoretically it's possible you might see a team emerge naturally and endure if its members gel and they see their problem or opportunity similarly. Possible, but unlikely, in my experience. Again, why? Two reasons.

One, real teams demand disciplines many people dislike. For example, team members must hold teammates accountable for their behaviour and results, not expect their leader to do it all. They must also accept their interdependence by giving up some autonomy.

Two, when adults try to achieve results together you can expect trouble at some point. When people work in teams, and especially when they feel under pressure, they create and unleash a complex array of hidden psychological forces. The result? Unhelpful behaviour. The effect is like balls bouncing around a snooker or pool table, cannoning into one another, creating chaos, misdirection and unintended results. These hidden forces mean you can't expect a bunch of adults to act as a team and achieve ambitious aims just because someone asks them to work together or they seem socially compatible.

In my view, the second issue – the psychological challenge – is the key factor because it's also the main driver behind reason one: team members' reluctance to accept interdependence and apply the discipline of joint accountability. So the first step in building successful teams is to understand the hidden psychological forces.

The rest of this chapter outlines these forces, drawing on what I call my Dual Forces model. I'm paring the content down to its essentials because my only aim here is to support the chapter's main point: it takes conscious effort to build teams.

I'm aware some readers will want greater detail as the Dual Forces model offers perhaps the fullest, clearest description of teams' psychological complexities for decades. If you do want a deeper understanding, I suggest you skip to this book's appendix, *The Hidden Psychology of Teams*, before returning to chapter 4. It offers greater detail on the dual forces, extra examples, mini case studies and technical notes. If you don't, read on for just the basic points.

Working in Teams Creates Anxiety

While coaching teams, I sometimes ask members to score their assertiveness on a 0–10 scale. Zero means they are poor at saying what they want, when they want, how they want, and getting the response they want, while ten means they are good at asserting themselves. I give them two scenarios. First, they rate their assertiveness when working *one-to-one*. Then we add their individual scores. Next, I ask them to repeat the 0–10 self-scoring, but this time rating their personal assertiveness when *working in a team*. Again, we add their scores.

Guess which total is always lower. It's "the working in a team" score. Repeatedly, I notice most people find it harder to express their thoughts and feelings genuinely and skilfully when working in teams and small work groups. They say the conditions feel riskier than one-to-one working, causing them to experience a subtle but real anxiety that cramps their style.

Dual Forces

Why? Why does working in teams and small groups make us uneasy and limit our contribution? It's because we're affected by dual forces. I call them the "Individual" and "Collective" forces.

- *Individual* forces flow from each member's mind.
- *Collective* forces stem from pressures created jointly by the members.

You might be thinking, "Isn't there another force coming from beyond the team, like company culture or pressure from competitors or perhaps the board of directors?" While it's true those external pressures do exert an influence, I don't include them as a third force because their effect is filtered and controlled by the Collective forces. That is, how the team as a whole views those outside sources, not the sources themselves. What controls the way they view them? The members' beliefs, notably their shared sense of team identity, purpose, values and capability. Together, they create the mental filter I call the team's "story", which we'll study in the next section. The point for now is that this collectively held set of beliefs presses in on their individual minds.

For example, members of a football team striving to win the English Premier League may lack belief in their ability to be champions. Now imagine a referee awards a questionable penalty against them. Their shaky self-belief causes them to see the referee's verdict as unjust and themselves as

Figure 1: Dual Forces Model
Individual and Collective Forces in Teams & Groups

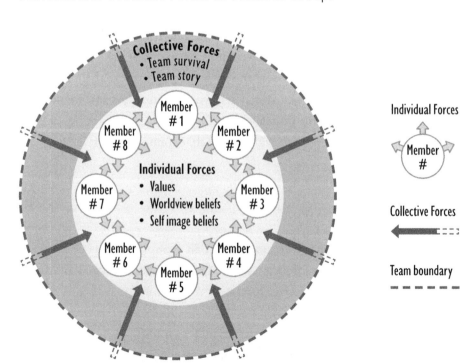

victims. Their sense of victimhood magnifies their fragile self-belief, which drives a dip in their mental toughness and energy, and they end up losing. Now imagine another football team with deeper self-confidence aiming for the same trophy and, again, imagine a referee's doubtful penalty award goes against them. They also see his ruling as unjust, but their greater belief in themselves spurs them to increase their efforts... and they win.

The message? It's the same external event, but the team's collective attitude decides if and how it affects their play. So external events by themselves don't create the forces acting on teams. Instead, the team members create Collective forces through their perception of external events. Without realising, they create a shared psychological filter that presses in on them from outside their individual minds.

Note that I'm saying forces plural. The Collective and Individual forces have their own sub-forces. The Collective forces comprise the *story* and *survival* sub-forces. The Individual forces encompass three sub-forces: the members' limiting *values*, their limiting *worldview* beliefs and their limiting *self-image* beliefs. You can see all five sub-forces in figure 1. We'll look at them in the next two sections and see how they combine to create an effect I call the Emotional Combustion Chamber. To echo what I wrote earlier, if you want to grasp the dual forces in greater depth, read the appendix, *The Hidden Psychology of Teams*.

Collective Forces

When team members repeatedly meet and work together, often without realising, they create expectations, mindsets, norms of thinking and behaviour, emotional bonds and habits. These combine to form a *living system*. This living system gives birth to the two Collective forces.

Note the term "living system" because both words are significant. A *system* arises when its elements interact to make a whole with a distinct identity and purpose that's greater than the sum of its parts. In other words, if you studied the parts separately you couldn't predict the system's characteristics and potential. So, for example, a car is a system. Cars contain assemblies like engines, gearboxes and dashboard computers, and tiny components like screws and rivets, but what makes them cars is the way the parts work together to create a means of transport with a distinctive look and feel. The parts can't do that separately.

Teams and groups are also systems. Their members are the parts. When they interact they create, influence and preserve the system. But groups and teams aren't mechanical systems, they're *living* systems. Like all living systems they do whatever they can to adapt and survive.

As the team members talk, they gain a measure of their colleagues, which is when relationships start to form. Consciously or unconsciously they build a sense of who they are collectively (identity), what they stand for (values), what they want to achieve and why (purpose), and what they're capable of – which, together, I call their *story* (the first of the two Collective forces). We can show it like this:

Team **story** = its shared sense of **identity**
+ **purpose**
+ **values**
+ **capability**

The "story force" spawns shared attitudes, beliefs, thinking habits and behavioural norms that, together, we call culture.

From this the living system (team) creates its second force: the drive to *survive*. Now the living system wants to survive and live out its story.

This is when the two Collective forces grow in strength. Now the combination of story and survival drives influences what the members think, feel and do, especially under pressure But this adds a twist to the team's culture. Although individuals unwittingly combine to create the living system, the system can, without them realising, come to control them by distorting the culture, driving their behaviour in unexpected ways.

Having understood the living system at high level, we'll look closer at the "story" and "survival" forces to see how they influence the team members' behaviour.

Figure 2: The Two Collective Forces

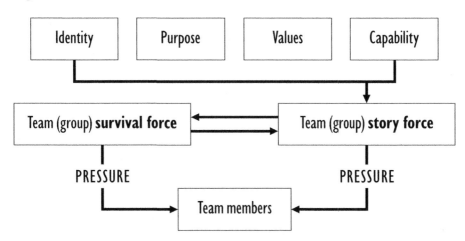

Story force

The first Collective force, the team's "story", has powerful effects. As you see in figure 2, identity, purpose, values and capability combine to form a mental model – a story – that a team's members subconsciously absorb, accept and play out in action. The story can develop quickly (within minutes) or slowly (over decades). Similarly, its effects can recede quickly or persist for years. I'll give you examples of the four components:

- *Identity:* "we represent this city", "we stand for this cause", "we're the good guys fighting the evil they represent", "we are the senior leadership team".
- *Purpose:* "we're aiming to win the championship", "we'll crush the enemy", "we'll launch this new product on time", "we've got to save this business".
- *Values:* "no finger-pointing, we succeed or fail as a team", "the end justifies the means", "no egos, everyone matters here", "customer satisfaction before everything", "maximising shareholder value is our top priority".
- *Capability:* "we can win this race", "we can do this task", "we're at our best when the pressure is on", "we're good but not good enough to win", "we have no chance".

An uplifting team story can be enormously helpful to a team's results. That's why crafting a positive story is one piece of the 7P team building model in Book Two (you'll read about it in chapter 17 on Group Unity). However, problems arise when teams and groups develop negative stories that grip them at certain moments – usually times of heightened emotion. This can cause two unhelpful effects.

One, groups may behave aggressively in ways their members wouldn't consider if they were acting on their own. For example, think of a lynch mob bent on killing someone on the spot unlawfully. The mob may hold the target responsible for a serious crime even if the person has done nothing wrong. The mob focuses on the target simply because he or she belongs to the "wrong" group – perhaps they have the "wrong" skin colour or practise the "wrong" religion. The lynch mob's identity ("we are against them"), purpose ("we must kill them to remove the threat they represent"), values ("the end justifies the means") and capability ("we can do it now if we act together") creates enough momentum and anonymity for its members to overcome any moral doubts and act as one to carry out the execution.

Two, they may perform well below their ability when facing pressures that play on their story fears. It could be a one-off below-par display, like a sports team "freezing" in a final. But if the story spreads and remains unchallenged, it can endure for years. I believe England's football team underachieved for decades because of its unspoken "story". Despite hosting the world's richest football league, England performed poorly in World and European championships, winning only 6 knockout round games in finals in the 50 years up to 2016. Even more striking in those 50 years was England's dire record in penalty shootouts – the moment when individual players must hold their nerve. It won only 14% of these "sudden death" contests, putting it 30th in the world for success at shootouts, well below its average team ranking (10th) over that half-century. This dismal long-term picture reached its peak when Iceland, with a population of 330,000, the tiniest nation ever to reach the European finals, fought back from 1–0 down to outplay England and knock them out of the 2016 tournament. Until 2016, I suspect England teams saddled themselves with a story containing a destructive capability belief. The story may have been: "We're the nation that invented football so English fans expect us to do well (*identity*), therefore we'll do our best (*purpose*) but we're not good enough to handle tough moments in knockout games (*capability*) and when we fail they'll condemn us." Alongside the corrosive capability belief ("not good enough"), note the watery purpose ("we'll do our best"). Note too the absence of values to give the players pride, energy and belief when joining the national squad. If you're interested, there's more data on this example in the appendix, *The Hidden Psychology of Teams*.

Survival force

I've been explaining that a group's members may yield to the system's pressure to live out its story by thinking and behaving in certain habitual ways. In this way they can lose their individual ability to choose freely and start reacting to events in ways they wouldn't do outside the team or group. The "survival" force can have a similar effect (often on an even wider scale) whenever the group feels threatened and its continued existence is in question.

Think about the behaviour of the Roman Catholic Church in the last five decades. Despite its Christian message, some priests molested and raped young parishioners in secret. When victims complained, what did the Church do? It went into survival mode. Bishops told themselves the church's image came first and justice second. Thus began a worldwide cover-up. Yet this ran counter to the Church's spiritual mission and morals. Why did it happen? Because the living system's survival drive – its second Collective force – was controlling individuals' behaviour.

The Roman Catholic Church is an extreme but not unique example of the survival force at work. Consider the 2016 FIFA (football's world governing body) scandal where executive after executive tumbled from power with whistle-blowers and investigators exposing their fraud, cover-ups and false denials, which they'd justified to themselves as "protecting FIFA". The living system's pressure to survive caused individuals and even groups within FIFA to become stuck in foolish or disgraceful behavioural patterns.

The point is that through the survival force living systems can mimic Doctor Frankenstein's monster, meaning the creation becomes the oppressor, as happened in Mary Shelley's famous novel. Thus, the members yield to the living system's drive to survive. They do things external observers can see, but those inside cannot. Even if a minority do, they often feel powerless to change things because the urge to survive as a collective entity dominates the group's thinking.

Collective forces' effect on work teams

How do Collective forces typically show at work in leadership and project teams? You normally see them when team members feel apprehensive. The team feels under pressure or threatened. Perhaps their results are poor or they're tackling a high-risk project or face external criticism. That's when the story and survival forces kick in, pressing in on the members.

Research and observation shows they may respond in one of six ways. The first four are survival-driven. The fifth flows from either the story or survival drives or a combination of both. The sixth occurs when teams out-play their negative story. I'll outline the six ways briefly. You'll find fuller explanations, with examples, in this book's appendix, *The Hidden Psychology of Teams*.

1. **Over-dependence on the leader:** Where members over-rely on a charismatic leader to solve their problems and survive. Leader dependency blocks real team formation.

2. **Leader scapegoating:** To help the team survive the followers blame the dominant but failing leader while absolving themselves ("these problems aren't my fault"). Meanwhile attention to task performance slips amid the upheaval and search for a new leader.

3. **Avoidance of issues:** A result of members' subconscious urge to keep the team intact and survive by avoiding conflict at almost any cost. Members will skirt around issues they should tackle and avoid bold decisions, but the delay makes the unresolved issues worse.

4. **Groupthink:** Like "avoidance", the aim is group togetherness and survival. Unlike avoidance, instead of fudging issues and delaying decisions, the team signs up to bold goals or plans

some members quietly disagree with but won't challenge, often with disastrous results for the team. Others may discourage colleagues from expressing opposing views or even withhold important evidence that would challenge the team's aims and plans. Two examples of groupthink I've described in the appendix are the 1961 Bay of Pigs fiasco and the Royal Bank of Scotland's (RBS) takeover of ABN-Amro in 2007.

5. **Focus on external enemies:** This prevents the team from splintering by creating a temporary unifying force centred on external dangers, real or imagined. But by persisting in focusing on external enemies, members may drain their energy, become paranoid, and lose sight of their original aims. It may also lead to denial, cover-ups and aggressive lethal action. Also, gripped by paranoia, a team's idea of "enemies" may widen to include other parts of its parent organisation, reducing cooperation and harming overall results.

6. **Collective fragility under pressure:** This stems from a team's shared belief in a potent negative "story" about its joint capability, e.g. "we can't win". Talented members who perform well in other circumstances can crumble under the fear generated by this Collective "story" force and execute poorly when facing situations they fear most.

Collective forces summary

To summarise, Collective forces appear when teams and groups develop a shared identity, purpose, values, and sense of capability that spawns shared norms, opinions and behaviours. From all this, living systems emerge that want to survive and enact their "story".

When teams and work groups feel under pressure, the survival drive (the second Collective force) or the negative story (the first Collective force) starts affecting their unwitting creators. These Collective forces show up in six ways: (1) leader over-dependency (2) leader scapegoating (3) a focus on external enemies (4) avoidance of issues (5) groupthink and (6) collective

Figure 3: Collective Forces & Behavioural Results

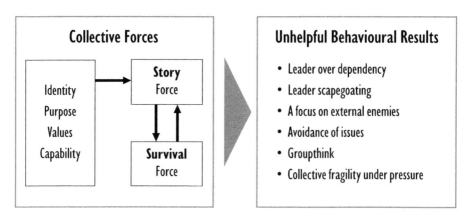

fragility. All six have unhelpful effects on teams' performance under pressure as illustrated in figure 3.

Individual Forces

The Collective forces are joint creations but the Individual forces emerge separately from each member's distinctive subconscious beliefs. To be more exact, from three types of beliefs: worldview beliefs, self-image beliefs and certain values. (Values are just a special class of beliefs.) To be more accurate still, from their specific *limiting* worldview beliefs, *limiting* self-image beliefs and *limiting* values. These are the three Individual sub-forces. They lead to unhelpful emotions and behaviour, increasing the complexity and challenge of working in teams. I've depicted this in figure 4.

Beliefs are ideas we judge to be true. Values are special beliefs in that they not only feel true, they guide what we think matters most in life. But not every belief or value we hold is true or helpful. Limiting beliefs – two of the three Individual forces – are neither true nor helpful. They are negative false subconscious ideas we have about our self-image, our abilities, life and other people that we assume are real. Limiting values are a bit different. Unlike beliefs, we can't always rate them on a true-versus-false scale but they're unhelpful to team cohesion and results as I'll shortly explain.

Figure 4: Components of Individual Forces

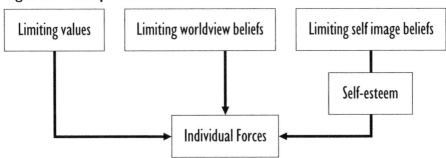

Limiting worldview beliefs

Three common limiting worldview beliefs contribute to the first Individual force:

The key worldview limiting beliefs	• "Others don't share my standards of workmanship; they'll let me down." • "You can't trust anybody; they'll only take advantage of you." • "People in power have special privileges; I mustn't challenge them."

They're the three I've found have the greatest effect on people's behaviour in small work groups. They affect people in different ways. For example: (1) Refusing to delegate. (2) Leaders rejecting colleagues' help even when they need it. (3) Being reluctant to say what we're really thinking and feeling to teammates for fear of being manipulated, hurt, rejected, punished or ostracised. (4) Refusing to use our initiative or contribute without instructions from senior figures because we believe we don't have the right to act or fear criticism from above.

Limiting self-image beliefs

I've found these (or versions of them) are the three most common limiting self-image beliefs affecting people's behaviour in teams:

The key self-image limiting beliefs	• "I'm insignificant; no one's interested in my opinion here." • "I'm not good enough; I'll only fail or make mistakes." • "I'm unlikeable; no one will ever trust me or feel close to me."

This second class of Individual forces has a huge influence over our thoughts, feelings and actions in teams.

For example, if we believe we're not good enough, we'll be afraid of failing or making a mistake or admitting there's something we don't know or understand. Why? Because we fear the humiliation we assume these experiences will guarantee. If instead we think we're unlikeable, we fear rejection by our colleagues if we say what we're really thinking or feeling and reveal the "real us". And if we believe we're insignificant, what do we fear most? Being ignored. Why? Because that will only confirm what we already "knew" (or rather believed) – that we're a nobody. And that will feel unbearably painful.

These fears are so unpleasant we seek ways to nullify the threats. That's when we create subconscious defence mechanisms. These are thinking, feeling and behavioural habits designed to ensure we don't meet the conditions we're most afraid of. Unfortunately the defences show as repeated (I stress that, repeated) unhelpful behaviour in teams – behaviour that blocks the team's success.[7] There are at least a dozen examples – and I'll list all of them in the summary table at the end of this section – but here are the first three examples: (1) avoiding or turning up late for meetings; (2) not speaking up at meetings; (3) hidden agendas.

Limiting values

Values define what matters to us in choosing priorities and actions. We hold values in numerous areas of our lives, but from the angle of unhelpful behaviour in teams, research highlights three values of interest:[8]

Key Limiting Values	Associated Beliefs
Low conscientiousness	"It's not important to give my best in every task I undertake; I don't care about doing tasks well or on time."
Low organisational citizenship	"I'll do what I'm paid to do and that's it; I've no interest in helping the company over and above my specific job duties."
Individualism over collectivism	"My priorities are more important than the team's – if I have to make a choice, I'll always look after number one first."

All three values, individually or together, can cause an unhelpful effect called "social loafing". "Social loafing" is where individuals contribute less work in a team than they would working solo, meaning the team's results are below the combined potential of its members, otherwise known as the 2+2 = 3 effect. Loafing members tell themselves, "We have enough people here to do the job, I'll let the others do the work and take a backseat." Social loafing is common. I've done it and I'll bet you have too. The appendix, *The Hidden Psychology of Teams*, offers more detail on social loafing if you're interested.

Individual forces summary

To bring everything together in this section on Individual forces, figure 5 shows examples of the common individually-driven behavioural problems you'll see in teams.[9] The behaviours I've listed are widespread. They are not extreme, rare or unusual. I suspect you'll have seen all of them at some time. There's a good chance you've committed some of them.

Figure 5: Individual Forces & Behavioural Results

Team Members' Individual Forces

Key Worldview Beliefs

"Others don't share my high standards; they'll only let me down."
"You can't trust anybody; they'll only take advantage of you
"I mustn't challenge the authority of people in power."

Key Self Image Beliefs

"I am not good enough; I'll fail or make mistakes."
"I am unlikeable; no one will like or trust me."
"I am insignificant they won't listen to me."

Key Values

"I don't care about doing tasks well or on time."
"I'll do what I'm paid to do and that's it; I won't help the company over and above my specific job duties."
"My priorities matter more than the team's I'll always look after number one first."

Unhelpful Behavioural Results

- Leaders under delegating / micromanaging
- Leaders rejecting colleagues' help
- Members not saying what they're really thinking and feeling (elephant in the room).
- Social loafing or refusing to take the initiative.
- Repeatedly avoiding meetings.
- Repeatedly turning up late for meetings.
- Repeatedly not speaking up at meetings.
- Hidden agendas.
- Sullen body language.
- Pairing up / cliques.
- Repeated finger pointing.
- Power struggles.
- Leaders crushing opposition or debate.
- Leaders avoiding responsibilities.
- Saying one thing but doing another (sabotage)
- Members not delivering on their promises.

These behaviours aren't always created by Individual forces. Other influences like poor chairing of meetings or an uninspiring team purpose can also drive them. But singly or combined, the left-hand panel's beliefs and values can cause all sixteen behaviours in the right-hand panel. All we need to grasp here are the many problems Individual forces can cause. If you wish to see the specific link between each behaviour and its controlling Individual forces, you'll find the detail in the appendix, *The Hidden Psychology of Teams*.

The point is that Individual forces can and do create at least sixteen unhelpful behaviours that make life in teams and small work groups more difficult. If you ignore them, they'll block a team's success.

The Emotional Combustion Chamber

What happens when the Collective and Individual forces come together? They create what I call the "emotional combustion chamber" shown in figure 6.

Figure 6: Dual Forces Create Emotional Combustion Chamber

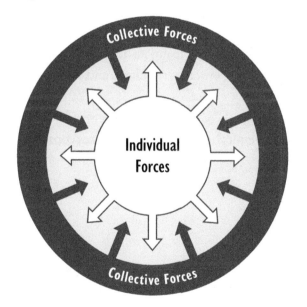

Collective Forces
- Team story
- Team survival

Individual Forces
- Individual limiting values
- Individual worldview limiting beliefs
- Individual self image limiting beliefs

Team members' operating space becomes an "emotional combustion chamber"

You'll find combustion chambers in petrol, diesel or jet engines. They're where fuel and air are mixed, put under pressure and ignited to create the controlled continuous explosions that propel cars and jets forward. Controlled explosions are, of course, what you want in cars and jets. But teams don't set out to create such fiery conditions. However, that's what unbridled interplay of the Collective and Individual forces will produce.

By using the "emotional combustion chamber" metaphor I'm not suggesting teams are always on the point of exploding. But I am saying the two forces' combined effect can produce charged atmospheres with hidden undercurrents and agendas that confuse, discourage or demotivate team members. Hence my earlier metaphor of snooker balls cannoning into one another. That's when misunderstandings occur and get-togethers become boring, frustrating and fruitless or, alternatively, tense and unpleasant. The ultimate effect on the team's performance? You'll see five possibilities, all unwanted:

- Important decisions avoided.
- Poor decisions made.
- Low creativity.
- Excessive or insufficient risk-taking.
- Poor execution, especially under pressure.

There's one more potential result. If it's the top team, its behaviour will set a bad example to others, damaging morale, lowering standards and slowing (or blocking) progress.

What I'm saying is that if you ignore these forces or leave them unchecked, you'll end up with these unwanted results because, I repeat, it takes conscious effort to create teams.

Conclusion

This chapter's psychological detail is helpful, but you needn't remember it all, just the overall message: *teams exert powerful psychological forces on us as members, causing unhelpful behaviour, making it harder to work together.* Thus, groups don't become teams by accident. It takes insight, skill, effort, time and practice to sidestep the negative Individual and Collective forces and create a cohesive, strong-willed, creative team that doesn't buckle under pressure. Helping you gain this insight and skill is the main aim of How To Build Winning Teams Again and Again.

Insight is where we start. Chapters 4 and 5 will describe the important differences between groups and teams. Chapter 6 will explain why few senior management groups become real teams. Chapters 7–9 outline a model to help you and your colleagues figure out what's going on *while you are in the thick of the psychological fog created by the Collective and Individual forces.* This prepares the ground for the practical parts of the trilogy in Books Two and Three.

The Key Points...

- Most people find it harder to express themselves in teams and groups than when they work one-to-one. The reason? Working in teams often creates anxiety. Why? Because two sub-conscious psychological forces are at work. They create an emotional combustion chamber, triggering chaotic conditions which, in turn, make it harder for groups to become real teams.

- The two are the *Collective* forces and *Individual* forces.
  - Collective forces stem from pressures created jointly by the team members. You could say they *press in* on team members from outside their individual minds.
  - Individual forces flow from each team member's psyche. You could say they *press out* from their individual minds onto other team members.

- Both have their own sub-forces. The Collective force is made up of the *story* and *survival* sub-forces. The Individual force encompasses three sub-forces: the members' limiting *values*, their *worldview* limiting beliefs and their *self-image* limiting beliefs.

- When team members repeatedly meet and work together, they develop a distinct identity, sense of purpose and capability, and values. From these, the team's *story* unfolds, resulting in a living system. Being a living system, it wants to *survive* and live out its story.

- Although the members create the Collective forces, usually without realising, the living system they create comes to behave like Doctor Frankenstein's monster. That's when the forces oppress the members, making them conform to the story and need to survive. This can cause the members to behave incompetently, illegally or immorally ... or well below their combined potential. In teams at work you'll often see the survival and story forces expressed in six ways when members feel fearful – perhaps because results are poor or they're tackling a high-risk, high-stakes project or they face external criticism. They are:
  1. Leader over-dependency.
  2. Leader scapegoating.
  3. Avoidance of issues.
  4. Groupthink.
  5. Focus on external enemies.
  6. Collective fragility.

- The Individual force's limiting beliefs stem from negative self-images and worldviews. Its limiting values centre on conscientiousness, organisational citizenship and individualism. Singly or combined, these limiting beliefs and values can cause sixteen unhelpful behaviours:
  1. Leaders under-delegating, over-controlling or micromanaging.
  2. Leaders rejecting help even when they need it.
  3. Members not saying what they're really thinking or feeling.
  4. Refusing to use our initiative and creativity OR social loafing.
  5. Repeatedly avoiding meetings.
  6. Repeatedly turning up late for meetings.
  7. Repeatedly not speaking up at meetings.
  8. Working to hidden agendas (concealed clashing motives).

9. Sullen body language.

10. Pairing up and cliques.

11. Repeated finger-pointing.

12. Power struggles.

13. Leaders crushing opposition or debate.

14. Leaders ducking responsibilities, e.g. decisions or removal of team members.

15. Saying one thing but doing another, what I call "executive sabotage".

16. Not delivering on promises.

- Combined, the Collective and Individual forces create an Emotional Combustion Chamber, triggering hidden undercurrents and agendas and chaotic behaviour. This only confuses, discourages or demotivates team members. If these forces are left unchecked, these are the likely results:

  1. Unproductive and perhaps unpleasant meetings.

  2. Members avoiding key decisions or instead making poor choices.

  3. Members losing their collective ability to solve big problems with fresh thinking.

  4. Sloppy execution of decisions or collective underperformance under pressure.

  5. Reckless risk-taking or its opposite, too little creative risk-taking.

  6. Top teams setting a bad example, damaging company morale and results.

- You needn't remember every idea in this chapter, just this one thought: *groups won't become real teams if you allow the Collective and Individual forces to run riot.* Putting it another way, groups don't become teams by accident. It takes insight, time and conscious effort to weaken or avoid the dual forces and build cohesive, strong-willed, creative teams that endure.

4

The Team Progression Curve

I said in chapter 3 that groups and teams are different so it's time to explain what I meant because you'll find it tougher to build and keep a real team going if you can't recognise one. The trouble is, you'll hear people refer to boards of directors, executive committees, sales forces, departments and whole companies as "teams". But calling something a team doesn't make it one. This habit of describing almost any small group as "a team" makes it harder to distinguish real teams, their disciplines and benefits. Besides, the action model in Book Two of this trilogy poses the question, "Do you need to act as a Performance Group or a Real Team?" so there's a practical reason for understanding the differences.

Small Groups in General

Let's start with the basics. A team is just one kind of small group. You can find smaller groups of many types: social groups, family groups, therapy groups, training groups and work groups. Teams are a subdivision of work groups.

Small work groups share two distinctive features: one, they exist chiefly to do a job and, two, they typically have 15 or fewer members. Everything we'll discuss from now on will focus on work groups.

The Team Progression Curve

You'll see three forms of small work groups: Task Groups, Performance Groups and Teams. Within that third category you'll meet four team types: Potential Teams, Pseudo Teams, Real Teams and High-Performance Teams.

We'll start with the big picture and then in the next chapter we'll zoom in on the two work groups that interest us most in this trilogy: Performance Groups and Real Teams. To put across the key points without getting lost in the detail, we'll use the Team Progression Curve. This depicts the six work groups in graphic form (figure 7).[10]

You'll see two axes on the graph: "team performance and impact" and "team unity". The higher the group or team's performance and impact – that is, the greater its resilience, creativity and results – the closer it is to the top of the graph. The more a group or team feels and acts as a united entity, the further to the right side of the graph it's shown.

Before continuing, I want to acknowledge Katzenbach & Smith's research

Figure 7: Team Progression Curve

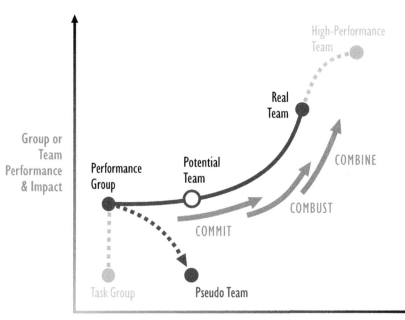

into teams nearly 30 years ago because the Team Progression Curve draws on their data and adapts a graph from their book, The Wisdom of Teams. I've introduced the terms "task group" and "performance group" and drawn the diagram differently from the curve they plotted, but they take credit for the underlying data and for introducing the labels "potential team" and "pseudo team". [11]

A Task Group (for example, a parish council, a social club committee or a charity's board of trustees) has low unity and performance. Task groups' duties change little over the medium term, say five years. They have a purpose, well-organised ways of working (perhaps quarterly meetings, pre-set agendas and sub-committees), the members meet and make decisions together and some may have clear roles, like Chair and Treasurer. They have tasks but don't need to keep improving their results in the face of competition. And individual members don't feel the pressures to deliver you find in the other work groups. That's because their mission is largely about upholding the status quo and sometimes because their roles are unpaid. Apart from governance committees you don't see many task groups in business. That's why Task Group is greyed out in the graph.

Performance Groups are also low in unity, but they perform better. That's because they have to. Like Task Groups, they have a job to do, but they or their organisations face greater pressure to improve results, often while fighting off competitors. Indeed, they're usually expected to improve results steadily year-on-year. Also, individual members face greater pressure to deliver their part of the work than members of Task Groups. Performance Groups follow a hub-and-spokes model. Members largely work apart to deliver results – because that's enough to achieve their goal – while the leader concentrates on coordinating and holding them accountable. They occasionally meet to make decisions and share data. Most so-called "management teams" and "leadership teams" in my experience are in fact Performance Groups. We can distil this portrayal of a Performance Group to a bite-sized definition:

> **A small group of people who set out to deliver against demanding performance standards by coordinating its individual members' contributions, without needing collective work outputs.**

A *Real Team* is different. It's more united and performs better. Much better in fact. Think of it as a Performance Group facing a tough challenge that's forced it to combine members' skills and experience to deliver results they couldn't achieve by working apart. Like solving an important problem. Or creating something new like designing a new car or figuring out a new company vision. Or jointly carrying out a plan. It still has a leader but it's climbed the curve by abandoning the hub-and-spokes model and addressing the three psychological team issues – Commit, Combust and Combine (we'll look at them in chapter 7) – to achieve extraordinary results other groups can't match. It can also offer its members a more fulfilling experience by tapping into three of the four intrinsic motivators: togetherness, the feeling they're learning and growing, and a strong sense of purpose.[12] Here's how I'd define a Real Team in one sentence:

> **A small group of people with complementary skills and roles who commit to a specific challenging common purpose, blend their abilities, and hold one another accountable for delivering collective work outputs and results.**

Emergency surgical teams and fire crews would be examples of Real Teams. So would military combat squads. High-profile examples in the business world include the teams designing, launching and honing Google's search engine in the late 1990s to early 2000s and Walt Disney's animation teams.

High-Performance Teams are just extreme versions of Real Teams. People often talk about them, but research shows they are rare, which is why I've greyed out the HPT position in figure 7's graph.[13] They differ from Real Teams in three ways. First, team members are exceptionally dedicated to supporting one another emotionally and professionally. Second, they show unusual devotion to the goal, which feels more like a cause. Third, they share leadership to the point where it's hard to tell who the leader is when they're in action. I'll say more about the characteristics of High-Performance Teams later in this chapter.

Here's the bad news: Katzenbach & Smith's research suggests you can't create High-Performance Teams on purpose. Why? Because there are no "secret sauces", models, methods or best practices for deliberately nurturing or guaranteeing the extraordinary degree of personal commitment High-Performance Team members display to one another. You cannot force team members to care deeply about one another's personal and professional success, emotional well-being and progress. It either grows organically or it doesn't. Thus, you could say real teams are *built*, but high-performance teams *emerge*.

The good news is that you can intentionally create Real Teams. When I work with clients who realise that acting as a Performance Group won't achieve their goals, we focus on helping them become a real team. In my view, it's the key position on the Team Progression Curve. My advice is to cherish High-Performance Teams if they arise, but don't expect them to happen. Aim for Real Team performance and enjoy the results.

What about the other two positions on the curve: Potential Teams and Pseudo Teams?

Potential Teams have figured out their number one goal and realise they're facing a challenge they can only handle by shifting from being a Performance Group to becoming a Real Team. They feel more "together" but they're only starting to climb the curve. They've made a mental transition because they realise they must change if they are to achieve something difficult and important, but they're only beginning their journey. A Potential Team finds itself in an interim phase, which is why, unlike the other positions, I've shown it as a light circle.

Pseudo Teams chase the idea of morphing from Performance Group to Real Team not because they face a challenge that demands they act as a team, but because members think it's a "good idea" or it's the "right thing to do". They call themselves a team while pursuing harmony above all else but achieve poor results. Why poor results? Because they focus solely on team-work. By "teamwork", I mean behaviours like listening, responding helpfully to others' opinions and offering emotional support. This promotes helpful conduct and boosts unity but doesn't create a team. You can recognise a real team by its performance challenge, the disciplines its members apply to one another and its outstanding results. Pseudo Teams lack all three. Even worse, they give Real Teams a bad name, for four reasons. One, they achieve little while wasting people's time. Two, they often give team members a frustrating experience, which lowers their individual productivity. Three, through their all-out attention to harmony, they lose the focus on outcomes they had as a Performance Group, and when their results dip, they start buck-passing and finger-pointing. Four, they discourage people from trying to build or engage in teams in the future. To bring this concept to life, I'll give you two examples of Pseudo Teams: one wasn't exposed for years while the other was unmasked in just over 12 months.

> The first was the leadership group of a company selling children's toys and games. The managing director told me, "We're a great team, we get on well. We visit the pub at lunchtimes for a pie and a pint and have a great laugh." He and his colleagues didn't realise that "getting on well" didn't make them a real team. They had no demanding shared performance goal. They didn't apply peer pressure to deliver and excel. They continued congratulating themselves on being a great "team" while their firm's financial results remained outstanding. But the profits weren't down to them. The market was buoyant and previous generations of managers had built strong consumer brand loyalty, so they lived off the fat of the land. For them, harmony was the teambuilding key, but the superficiality of their thinking remained unexposed while the financial numbers held up. If you assessed their added value as a team you would say their results were poor, but the profits disguised that reality for years … until their market faced a disruptive newcomer.

> Unlike the first example, this second Pseudo Team was soon exposed. A new work group running a £1 billion business, it comprised ten senior managers. Individually, they were capable. Together, they were a disaster. When I interviewed them, they told me how pleased they were by their friendliness, good humour and civility to one another. In digging deeper, I learned how frustrated they were at getting little done together, but they weren't admitting it among themselves. Their employees weren't fooled. They roundly criticised the senior "team's"

performance. As in the first example, there was no clear common performance goal. The members weren't pushing one another to deliver. Nor were they saying what they were thinking for fear of disturbing their meetings' friendliness and good humour. To external observers they appeared chummy with one another, but dissatisfaction and hostility lurked just below the surface. In the early days, it didn't matter as financial results were excellent. But as the months went by, they either avoided crucial decisions or made poor choices. After 12 months, employee engagement dipped and profits started to slide. Criticism rained down. Scapegoating within the "team" began and six months later, half of them were fired or reassigned. In their brief time as a Pseudo Team they'd done lasting damage to the business.

Getting Stuck On The Curve

I use this metaphor to sum up the Team Progression Curve: imagine a distant mountain rising sharply from a marshy plain, a bit like the north face of the Eiger. The marshy plain is the gap between Performance Group and Potential Team. Hidden in the marshes are treacherous patches of quicksand. The quicksand traps represent the Pseudo Team. You know the view from the summit (Real Team) is worth the effort of getting there, but you want to avoid the quicksand. The mountain's steepness symbolises the difficulty of shifting from Potential Team to Real Team.

On the point about steepness, here's the big problem: most would-be teams don't climb the curve to Real Team level. Why? Two possible reasons.

One, they fall into the Pseudo Team trap by assuming that getting along is the key to becoming a Real Team, meaning they practise "teamwork" behaviours like putting aside their egos, being caring and showing patience with colleagues. However, to repeat what I wrote a few paragraphs back, this promotes unity but doesn't create a team if there's no stretching performance challenge (especially no clear number one goal) and members don't apply team disciplines to one another.

Two, they get stuck at the Potential Team position and feel frustrated when their results disappoint. This heaps extra pressure on team members, making things worse.

The problem of getting stuck at the Potential Team position is central to this book. Katzenbach & Smith's research revealed five reasons for "stuckness":

Five Reasons for Getting Stuck at "Potential Team" on the Curve

Ignorance or non-application of the basics	The #1 reason. Not knowing or applying the basic disciplines for getting your group up the curve and keeping it there.
Members holding pessimistic beliefs about teams	Above all, the belief that teams don't perform better than individuals – that they're inefficient, a waste of time. They don't argue with the abstract notion of teams, but they have had off-putting experiences, creating bad memories. Perhaps because they were in a Pseudo Team, which is why I said earlier that pseudo teams can give real teams a bad name.
No distinctive purpose or goal, making team formation difficult	A common problem for senior leadership groups, who often assume their purpose is identical to the company's aims. This makes it hard (sometimes impossible) to define what they and they alone must deliver.
Some members fear being in a team	It gives them feelings of discomfort and risk. Maybe they fear being visible and speaking up with peers who can challenge them. Or they fear losing their freedom. Or they're uncomfortable listening to opposing viewpoints. Or they feel scared of peers holding them accountable in meetings.

The company lacks a compelling purpose or vision bringing significance and meaning to people's work	A powerful motivating company purpose usually creates a strong drive towards a high-performance ethos where employees expect a lot from themselves and colleagues, making it easier to form real teams. But its absence does the opposite: it can discourage or block real teams from forming. (NOTE: a ruthless *"top-down, do whatever it takes to hit the numbers"* attitude is not a high-performance ethos; it's a high-pressure ethos.[14] A high-performance ethos is about striving for excellence.)

The action model in Book Two of this series addresses the first four "sticky points". What about the fifth? Well, it's true that no wider, motivating company purpose can make life harder for everyone (unless they're the top team) because it's beyond their scope of influence. But it doesn't have to stop a team's successful formation – simply knowing about the fifth point can forewarn and forearm the team members.

Don't Confuse Teamwork with Teams

I've twice touched on the "teamwork" point already in this chapter, but it's worth expanding on. I'll be direct: the idea that teamwork is the key to building a team is false. Teamwork alone does not make a team.

"Teamwork" refers to collaboration and the values and behaviours supporting it. These include listening, keeping an open mind, responding helpfully to colleagues' views, speaking up when needed, supporting one another emotionally in tough moments, giving colleagues the benefit of the doubt and praising others' efforts. It also means being willing to use your time to serve the team (as in "she's a good team player"). In short, teamwork improves communication and unity, which is undoubtedly helpful.

But teamwork isn't exclusive to teams. Performance groups and task groups also need teamwork to succeed. Nor is it limited to small work groups as entire companies benefit from teamwork. Thus, "teams" and "teamwork" aren't synonymous. Yes, teamwork is necessary but it's not enough to form a team and deliver strong collective results. A team isn't just a united group of people who share the value of "teamwork". They are and they do, but the *context* must also demand a team, meaning the problem or opportunity has to be one that people can't address through solo efforts, however well-coordinated.

This is why offsite events focusing on teamwork alone often fail to transform performance groups into teams. Teamwork is only one ingredient in the teambuilding recipe. To repeat: you also need the *right context* plus certain disciplines for performance groups to become teams. What creates the right context? It's the team's *performance challenge expressed as a compelling goal that motivates all members.* This drives the need for teams and their disciplines. If in trying to become a team you stress teamwork and ignore the performance context and the disciplines it demands, you'll be friendly to one another, but you'll miss the real point: delivering a certain result.

A Closer Look At High-Performance Teams

In the next chapter we'll be concentrating on Performance Groups and Real Teams as they, especially the latter, are the focus of this trilogy but I mentioned earlier the research showing that High-Performance Teams are rare in the business world despite the term's widespread use. The data comes from Katzenbach & Smith's work. They judged that only 3 of the 47 executive teams they studied were high-performance teams. That's less than 7%.[15] Their data fits my experience – I've worked in just one high-performance team in 43 years.

One recent public example of a high-performance team is Leicester City football club, the 5000-to-1 winners of the English Premier League in 2016. They didn't have big name players, were among the favourites for relegation at the season's start and lacked the budgets of richer clubs. But through intense dedication to their teammates, superb organisation on the field, and sheer effort, they triumphed by eight points.

High-performance teams resemble real teams, but they deliver truly exceptional results because of three crucial differences. I listed them earlier, but here I'll give you more detail:

- First, the members feel unusually dedicated to teammates' support, success and personal growth. Katzenbach and Smith found that such commitments stretched outside the workplace and lasted beyond the team's lifespan. During research for this book, an American colleague told me this story about his experience in a high-performance team:

  "As a young man I played on a basketball team that went to the State Championship three consecutive years despite the school having less than one hundred students. But our coach knew how to build teams. What marked the unique nature of this team was the sense of lifelong connection between team members. Forty years after the glory days we had a reunion. By itself, that's not unusual. What was unusual was our conversations. They focused on how we were doing in non-economic terms. No size of house, salary, type of car driven or investments … just 'how are you doing?' on a purely human level."[16]

  High-performance team members not only push one another hard; they care about each other.
- Second, the members feel a sense of purpose that's bigger and far more important than their personal interests, to the point where it feels more like a cause than just a mission. At the extreme end – as in the case of an elite military team working behind enemy lines – it could be a cause the members feel is worth risking their lives for. Katzenbach and Smith noticed that high-performance team members always mentioned this part of their experience.
- Third, there'll be a formal leader, but the leader's status will be lower than you'll find in a real team because his or her teammates will more visibly share leadership responsibility. A high-performance team may consult its official leader before acting, but its members are more likely to seek approval from

whoever they see as the most qualified teammate in whatever situation they're facing. Martin Murphy, a former soldier in the British Army's Special Air Service (SAS) unit, which engages in highly classified counter-terrorism, hostage rescue and covert reconnaissance missions, had this to say on the subject:

"Hierarchy has a habit of being shunned in Special Forces and for good reason: ego gets involved [...] Anybody in a patrol could lead a mission dependent on experience and skills [...] Everyone is treated as an adult. Rank or position was not that important; skills and experience counted for more. Many an officer had his ear chewed off for presenting a rubbish plan by someone of lower rank. Sharing leadership duties makes everybody more empathetic [... because...] you've been on both sides of the coin so you tend to be more respectful, which boosts overall morale and performance."[17]

That's why if you watch a high-performance team in action you might struggle to identify the leader. You'd see everyone taking responsibility and several people playing the lead role in decision-making at different times.

Note that these three features are important for distinguishing high-performance teams from "high-performing teams". They sound identical but they're not. The latter are what I'd call successful real teams, but the former have moved up a level because they have developed the three features and are delivering superior results to match. Also, members of high-performance teams usually feel intense pride at being in the team. That's true both during the experience and afterwards. They retain strong favourable memories of their time in the team – notably the sense of fulfilment they felt and perhaps the fun they had.

There is, however, a rarely discussed "dark side" to life in high-performance teams. It can show in three ways. One, members may become so immersed that they overcommit to the experience, putting their health at risk. Two, it can permanently make or break their reputation with colleagues. Three, the team's intensity can develop a collective force – remember, we discussed collective forces in chapter 3 – causing misalignment with its parent company's aims or values. Professor Jerry Estenson, a former US Army captain who served in Project Delta 5th Special Forces Group in Vietnam as a reconnaissance team leader, had this to say about his covert combat experience and the advice he offers on team building courses:[18]

> "We felt a lot of pressure. It was partly a combination of the work's complexity (going behind enemy lines, sometimes over 100 miles, collecting intelligence and getting out without being discovered) and the risk (teams operated sterile, meaning no US Army uniforms, insignias or identification). But the pressure also came from the fact that the unit operated as a pure meritocracy. You couldn't lead a team unless its team members agreed to follow you. Rank had no value, just ability. That created extra pressure to perform. It also meant recon unit members could leave any time simply by asking – there was no stigma attached.
>
> One aspect of the "dark side" is that the pressure to perform pushed some people beyond their ability to keep going. That presented a challenge for leaders. How do you pull someone who doesn't know how to quit and values his membership in the unit beyond his personal well-being?
>
> The second element was "no forgiveness". That's best exemplified by a story about a book written about the unit. A retired officer conducted extensive research and put together a comprehensive account of the unit's history. Now you need to know that a newly promoted captain, an officer who later became Chairman of the Joint Chiefs of Staff, served with distinction in that unit. The author asked the General to write a short forward. After reading a proof of the book, the General said he couldn't help because part of it wasn't accurate. The part in question read something to the effect that, during the unit's history, the officers leading recon teams served well in those positions. The General said that wasn't always the case, pointing out that he'd removed two officers from team leadership roles.

My point is that those two young men didn't perform well in what was an unusual environment and even 40 years later they still weren't forgiven.

The comment I make when I teach high-performance team leadership courses is, 'Be careful how you construct and lead such teams. They will develop a culture of their own that can quickly become misaligned with the parent organisation. They will also set performance standards so high they will burn out team members. And people electing to join them need to know their lifelong reputation is being made on the team'."

Of course it's possible the "dark-side" experience is limited to undercover military high-performance teams. My advice is to stay alert to this "dark-side" risk if your real team happens to create enough intensity and unity to become one of the few making the transition to high-performance team.

The Key Points...

- The Team Progression Curve depicts six positions: Task Group, Performance Group, Pseudo Team, Potential Team, Real Team and High-Performance Team.

- A *Task Group* (e.g. a social club committee) has low unity and performance. It has a task but doesn't need to keep improving its results in the face of competition. Its members don't feel the pressures to deliver you find in the other work groups. Apart from governance-related boards or committees you don't see many Task Groups in business.

- *Performance Groups* are also low on unity, but they perform better. That's because they have to. Like Task Groups, they have a job to do, but they face greater pressure to improve results while needing to fight off competitors. They follow a hub-and-spokes model. Members largely work apart to deliver results (because that's enough to achieve their goal) while the leader concentrates on coordinating and holding them accountable. They occasionally meet to make decisions and share data. Most so-called "management teams" and "leadership teams" are in fact Performance Groups.

- A *Real Team* is different. It's more united and performs better. Much better in fact. Think of it as a Performance Group facing a tough challenge that's forced it to combine members' skills, experience and ingenuity to deliver results they couldn't achieve apart. Like solving an important problem. Or creating something new. Or jointly executing a plan. It still has a leader, but it's climbed the curve by abandoning the hub-and-spokes model and navigating the three psychological team phases – Commit, Combust and Combine (which we'll discuss in chapter 7) – to deliver superb results other groups can't match. High-profile examples include the animation teams at Disney and the people who created and launched Google.

- Thus, in a Performance Group, the sum of members' individual efforts is enough to deliver its aim. But that's not true in a Real Team because the goal is more demanding, meaning you need joint effort and ingenuity. So a Real Team is usually what you want when members' individual efforts cannot meet the goal even if skilfully coordinated by a single leader, usually because the challenge demands mindset changes, continuous innovation, a shift in ambition, urgent turnaround or a response to an external shock.

- *High-Performance Teams* are just extreme versions of Real Teams. They're often talked about, but research shows they're rare. They differ from Real Teams in three ways. First, team members are unusually dedicated to supporting one another. Second, they show extraordinary commitment to the goal (which feels more like a cause). Third, they share leadership even more than Real Teams – to the point where it's hard to tell who the leader is when they're in action.

- *Potential Teams* are in an interim phase. They have figured out their number one goal and realised they're facing a challenge they can only handle by becoming a Real Team, which is why they've shifted away from the Performance Group position. They feel more "together", but they're only starting to climb the curve.

- *Pseudo Teams* pursue high unity but only deliver worsening results. Why? Because they haven't shaped a motivating goal and in chasing harmony above all else they lose the results focus they had as a Performance Group. They often end in bouts of buck-passing and finger-pointing. Pseudo Teams can give Real Teams a bad name.

- It's important not to confuse "teamwork" with teams. Teamwork refers to collaboration and its underlying values and behaviours. Teamwork is helpful to team building, but it's not enough as you also need a demanding performance challenge requiring collective outputs and certain disciplines. And of course teamwork isn't specific to teams as it's also needed in Task Groups and Performance Groups. Indeed, entire companies benefit from teamwork.

- You can't create High-Performance Teams on purpose. That's because no one's discovered models, methods or best practices for deliberately nurturing or guaranteeing the extraordinary personal commitment that High-Performance Team members display to one another and their mission. It's not something you can force. They're not built; they emerge.

- However, you can deliberately create Real Teams. That's what I suggest clients aim for.

- Most work groups don't pass through the Potential Team phase and climb the curve to Real Team level. Typically, you'll see two reasons for this. One, they fall into the Pseudo Team trap. Two, they get stuck for one or more of the five reasons I listed on pages 58–59.

- High-Performance Teams are widely admired but for their members the intensity of the experience can have a dark side.

5

Performance Groups and Real Teams

In this chapter we'll put Performance Groups and Real Teams under the microscope as they, especially the latter, will be our focus from now on.

Differing Challenges of Performance Groups and Real Teams

If you understand the difference between the *challenges* that Performance Groups and Real Teams face, it becomes easier to grasp the basic team *disciplines*. So here we'll summarise those differing challenges. We'll explore the contrasting disciplines in the next section.

As you'll see in figure 8, Performance Groups largely share the first three challenges with Real Teams: pressure for results, pressure on individuals to deliver and, often, pressure from competitors. Their challenges start to diverge when we study rows 4–5, but the biggest divergence is on challenge #6, the bottom row. The sum of people's individual efforts is enough to deliver the Performance Group's aim, which means they don't need joint work results, they just have to focus on coordinating members' efforts and ensuring that group members stay motivated. But in Real Teams, the members' individual efforts aren't enough to meet the goal even if skilfully coordinated by a single leader. Why? Because *the challenge is more demanding as it typically needs*

Figure 8: Different Work Challenges

Challenges	Performance Group	Real Team
1. Pressure to improve overall results	Medium-High	High
2. Pressure on individuals to deliver	High	High
3. External competitors?	Often, not always	Often, not always
4. Performance expectations / emphasis	Steady gains in largely stable conditions	Rapid gains or sharp improvement
5. Challenge requires organisational change of some kind?	Not usually	Often
6. Challenge can be met by coordinating members' separate efforts?	Yes	No

change, innovation or sharp improvement in results, meaning that it demands joint effort and ingenuity. And that takes us neatly on to how the disciplines of Performance Groups and Real Teams differ.

Differing Disciplines of Performance Groups and Real Teams

For any work group to succeed, it needs to apply six basics. These are the six disciplines you'll find in any competent Task Group like a golf club committee. As you'll see in the lower part of the "Y" diagram in figure 9, all work groups must have:

- A clear enough purpose plus the rights and powers to achieve it.
- Clarity on who is and isn't a full group member.

Figure 9: Comparison of Three Work Groups' Disciplines

Performance Group Disciplines	Real Team Disciplines
Overall performance goal *equals* the sum of individuals' goals and efforts.	Overall performance goal exceeds the sum of individuals' goals and efforts.

Performance Groups & Real Teams

Performance Group Disciplines	Real Team Disciplines
1. Higher-pressure working approach shaped by a *single leader*.	1. Higher-pressure working approach shaped *by leader and members*.
2. Leader *presides over others' work*.	2. Leader *does real creative work*.
3. Members *assigned to individual tasks matching their skills*.	3. Members *work jointly to integrate complementary skills and talents*.
4. Results flow mostly *from individual members' efforts*.	4. Results flow *from joint effort, e.g. problem solving and creativity*.
5. Strong *individual* accountability.	5. *Joint and individual* accountability.

Task Groups

1. Clear purpose, rights and powers
2. Clear membership boundary
3. Good communication
4. Reasonably clear member roles
5. Time-efficient process
6. Reasonable accountability

Work Group Fundamentals

Adapted from a diagram in The Discipline of Teams by Jon Katzenbach & Douglas Smith, 2001

- Enough openness and listening between members.
- Defined roles for at least some members (so they know who's doing what).
- A way of working that gets things done without wasting much time.
- Members with enough sense of duty to carry out the group's task.

However, these basics aren't enough for Performance Groups and Real Teams. The left-hand fork of the Y shows the five extra disciplines that Performance Groups apply. You can see they add up to a tougher, more demanding setup than a Task Group's.

To remind you, Performance Groups can achieve their goals with leaders coaxing and coordinating individual efforts from their colleagues. Although the leaders often set the group's purpose and goals, they don't usually get involved in the work itself. They assign members to tasks that suit their skills and personalities, hold them individually accountable if they don't perform well, control the group's pace and apply a higher-pressure working approach and standard than you'll find in Task Groups. Leaders will use get-togethers to explain overall progress, ask members to brief one another, review data and nudge the group towards joint decisions. To give you an example of a Performance Group, consider golf's biennial Ryder Cup event between the USA and Europe. The captain of a Ryder Cup "team" – in reality, a performance group – chooses who will play, when and with whom, but success or failure depends largely on each golfer's results. Another example of a Performance Group would be a typical so-called senior management "team". Research by Katzenbach & Smith showed that few groups of managers, especially at senior levels, are real teams. I'll explain why this is so in the next chapter because I don't want to overlook the main point here: distinguishing between Performance Groups and Real Teams.

A Real Team applies the same six basic work group disciplines, but as you'll see in the right-hand fork of the Y in figure 9, it replaces the Performance Group's disciplines with five new ones. Why? Because, unlike the Performance Group, it can't achieve its aims with its members working largely on individual assignments, even if they perform to their maximum. This means you'll usually see these five differences in working approach between Real Teams and Performance Groups:

- First, although there may be an official team leader, he or she won't always assign the roles, choose the members and set the goals, pace and working approach. In other words, team leaders don't dominate leadership the way leaders in performance groups do. They may appoint members, but they'll usually agree the team's aims, working approach and pace with their colleagues. Thus, you'll see a degree of shared leadership that will vary according to whether the team has made it to Real Team status or gone further to attain the rare High-Performance Team position. Through shared leadership, team leaders ensure maximum commitment – one of a real team's hallmarks.
- Second, and just as important, team leaders typically do real creative work; they don't just preside over others, which is more common in Performance Groups.[19]
- Third, instead of doing much of their work apart, members will work together to plan, solve problems and create outputs (for example, a new software program or a new vision for the business or an emergency bridge across a river). They realise that individually they can't achieve what they want so they pool their talents, skills, knowhow and contacts to create a result they couldn't deliver separately, even with skilful coordination by the leader. This is different to performance groups who will meet to brief on progress, review data and make decisions, but won't do major creative or problem-solving work together. Instead they'll delegate such tasks to a sub-committee (which may need to act as a real team) or other colleagues outside the group.
- Fourth – and it's a result of the third discipline – the Real Team's results will mainly flow from its members joint work, not their solo efforts, whereas Performance Groups rely more on individual outputs.

- Fifth, in Real Teams, all members accept the need to perform well, a pressure they exert on and receive from one another. Team members hold themselves accountable for their own impact but they'll hold others accountable too. They won't wait for the leader to approve or reprimand a member for poor attitude, behaviour or results (which is what you'll normally find in Performance Groups); they'll do it themselves. You'll also notice that while team members hold themselves accountable for their own efforts and are ready to criticise underperforming colleagues, they also regard themselves as jointly accountable for the whole team's performance and overall results. As they see it, they succeed or fail as a team, meaning post-event scapegoating is out. This is what I mean by "joint and individual accountability", the fifth team discipline in the Y-diagram.

For example, imagine a dozen-strong group charged with designing a new car – that's an example of a real team. An eight-man elite Special Air Services (SAS) unit with a specific combat mission is also a team. Football or rugby teams obviously qualify as real teams. In short, to remind you of my earlier definition, a real team is:

> A small group of people with complementary skills and roles who commit to a specific challenging common purpose, blend their abilities and hold one another accountable for delivering collective work outputs and results.

To meet their challenge, team members blend their skills, experience and energy to create collective work outputs in pursuit of the aim. What do I mean by "collective work outputs"?

Let's start with what I *don't* mean. I exclude getting together to review, discuss, decide something and delegate tasks to others.

So what do I include? Imagine a football team completing a twelve-pass move from a defensive position to score a goal ... or a project team figuring out a new manufacturing process ... or a fire-fighting team rescuing a family from a burning block of flats ... or a leadership team executing an assimilation-integration project together following a merger or takeover. These are all examples of collective work outputs.

In business, I've seen these common examples of collective work outputs when working with clients:

- Crafting a new vision for their company or department.
- Designing a new product or service.
- Figuring out a plan to transform a company's culture.
- Analysing the company's strategic position together and drawing conclusions on the main problems and opportunities.
- Jointly delivering a transformational change programme.

In short, you will see collective work outputs any time two or more team members "roll up their sleeves" and create something, solve a problem, plan something, or execute change together.

The "Performance Group or Real Team?" Choice

It's true that Real Teams deliver better results while offering a more fulfilling experience. But they are harder to build and uphold than Performance Groups and you only need a team when group members can't reach the goal by working individually under a leader's guidance. Am I saying there are times when you don't need a team even when there's pressure to deliver better results? That's exactly what I'm saying. Indeed, you'll see moments when a Performance Group is the wiser choice.

That's why I often say to coaching clients, "Don't strive to become a Real Team unless your performance challenge demands it." By this, I mean that together you must deliver results you couldn't achieve working apart, even with your leader acting as coordinator. If you strive to become a team for ideological reasons, assuming "it's always the best answer", you are likely to fall into the Pseudo Team trap.

As a rule of thumb, choosing to work as a Performance Group makes sense when:

1. Your group's aims centre on (a) sharing data (b) sharing best practices (c) making and delegating decisions (d) setting and enforcing high standards of individual performance.

2. The total of your individual members' efforts will deliver what you want. In other words, you don't need collective work outputs, whether from people working together in one room or using video links.

3. You judge the risk of creating a Pseudo Team is higher than the gains you will realise from working as a Real Team, especially when the group faces overwhelming barriers to a team approach. For example, when there's a crisis and no time to form a team. Or there's a leader who doesn't believe in the power of teams and won't share control. Or if the group has cynical, stubborn, difficult members who won't accept team disciplines and you can't replace or work around them.

The advantage of Performance Groups is that you needn't jump through the hoops of becoming a Real Team. You don't have to spend time becoming accustomed to greater sharing of leadership, building high trust levels, getting used to holding one another to account, giving up some autonomy, adapting to interdependence, and learning to accept that the team's aims come before yours. All this takes hard work, candour and usually some conflict, which can bruise egos. It may also divert team members from their day job.

That said, Performance Groups don't work so well when faced with difficult but common challenges like:

- Leading major change in a company's priorities, working practices, culture or atmosphere.
- Innovation in products, services or work processes.
- Fast responses to competitors' moves, technological shifts, huge changes in government regulations or market shocks.
- Urgent creative or problem-solving projects.

Why? Because Performance Groups aren't geared for the degree of initiative, cooperation, creativity, shared leadership, conflict and pressure needed to handle such demanding challenges. When you face tests like these, a decision to work as a Real Team makes sense. The key, therefore, is to make a *deliberate choice* between acting as a Real Team or a Performance Group based on the challenge you and your colleagues are facing. The practical questions to ask are:

1. Are we looking to achieve a result a Performance Group can't deliver?
2. Will our attitudes – especially the leader's – allow us to apply team disciplines?
3. Are we prepared to put in the hard work to grow into a Real Team? That is, handling the inevitable conflicts, putting effort into mutual trust-building, and being ready to swap interdependence for solo working.

If the answers are "yes", "yes" and "yes", a Real Team approach looks a good choice.

It's Not A One-Time Choice

I've said repeatedly that deciding to act as a Performance Group or a Real Team is not a matter of ideological preference. It depends, above all, on your goal because that decides how much of your work will be collective. However, *this doesn't mean the Performance Group versus Real Team choice is a permanent one*. Yes, your challenge and its associated tasks may demand that you work as a Real Team, but once you've achieved your goal you can revert to handling your more individual (less collective) tasks while acting as a Performance Group.

Knowing the choice isn't permanent leads to a second conclusion: *if you master the Real Team disciplines, you can consciously switch to acting as a Performance Group when you want to so*. You'll need to gain experience in working as a Real Team to switch successfully, but once you've done so, it's doable. Obviously, if you've only worked as a Performance Group, switching won't be possible. This means people have the wrong idea if they ask, "Are we a team?" or announce, "We are a Performance Group" or "We are a Real Team". The question is not what you are or want to be. It's what you're *acting as* and, more important, what you need to *act as*. Grasp that and you will realise the

Performance Group versus Real Team choice isn't forever, it is situational.

Here's an example of what I mean. Some years ago, I coached the CEO of an $10 billion international company and his senior group. Reporting to him were six business unit presidents and six department heads, including the Finance, Human Resources and R&D chiefs. A manufacturing company, it owned businesses around the world with few obvious product or market overlaps. The CEO and his colleagues worked as a performance group, not a team. They followed the hub-and-spokes model with the CEO as the hub and his twelve colleagues as the spokes. The group met once a month for an hour, with the six business unit presidents joining by video or phone. Typically, they spent 30 minutes sharing financial and health, safety and environmental results and the remaining half-hour on a chosen "hot topic", reviewing progress and discussing best practice – for example, explaining what they were doing to improve on-time delivery to customers. The CEO also held one-to-one meetings with each direct report to dive deeper into selected topics.

Why did they work this way? Because they felt they were running a holding company as they hadn't seen obvious product-market links between their business units. Just as important, the CEO didn't want to waste his business unit presidents' time by adopting bigger agendas demanding longer or more frequent meetings. (He feared falling into the Pseudo Team trap.) He preferred meeting monthly for short sharp data-sharing meetings, leaving deeper dives to one-to-one conversations. For him, this was a rational, time-efficient answer.

But at a team coaching session they saw the need to transform their worldwide business with a cultural change programme. They realised this meant working on tasks requiring them to work as a real team. However, when they gathered for their old-style monthly meetings – which continued in parallel with their culture change efforts – they chose to carry on working as a performance group. They had to learn to work as a real team, but afterwards they deliberately switched between the two disciplines, depending on how they needed to act. If they'd stayed in performance group mode they wouldn't have achieved their cultural change goal. But if they'd stayed in real team mode, their monthly meetings would have become time-wasting and frustrating, especially for the business unit presidents calling in by phone and video.

The Key Points...

- The Team Progression Curve depicts six positions: Task Group, Performance Group, Pseudo Team, Potential Team, Real Team and High-Performance Team.

- *Performance Groups* face greater pressure to improve results than Task Groups while needing to fight off competitors. They follow a hub-and-spokes model. Members largely work apart to deliver results (because that's enough to achieve their goal) while the leader concentrates on coordinating and holding them accountable. They occasionally meet to make decisions and share data.

- *Real Teams* are different. They're more united and perform better. Much better in fact. Think of them as Performance Groups facing tough challenges forcing them to combine members' skills, experience and ingenuity to deliver results they couldn't achieve apart. Like solving an important problem. Or creating something new. Or jointly executing a plan. They still have leaders, but they've climbed the curve by abandoning the hub-and-spokes model and navigating the three psychological team phases – Commit, Combust and Combine (which we'll discuss in chapter 7) – to deliver superb results other groups can't match.

- Performance Groups and Real Teams both apply the six basic disciplines of any work group: (1) Clear purpose plus the rights and powers to achieve it. (2) Clarity around who is and isn't a full group member. (3) Enough openness and listening between members. (4) Defined roles for at least some members so they know who's doing what. (5) A way of working that gets things done without wasting time. (6) Members with enough sense of duty to carry out the group's task.

- However there are key differences in the ways Performance Groups and Real Teams work.

  - A skilled *Performance Group* applies the six basic disciplines and adds five more. The official leader – who presides over the other members – assigns them to tasks suiting their skills and personalities, holding them individually accountable if they don't perform well (because results mostly flow from individuals' efforts) and controls the group's pace, ensuring rigorous working standards. He or she may also set the group's purpose and goals, but not always. It's a tougher more demanding setup than a task group.

  - A winning *Real Team* applies the same six basics but replaces the performance group's five extra disciplines with five of its own. Like a performance group, it will set demanding working standards, but the team as a whole decides what those standards should be ... and may also set its goals. In this way there's greater sharing of leadership. Leaders are expected to do real work, not simply preside. Results flow more from joint work and pooling of skills. Finally, there isn't just individual accountability, there's joint accountability – meaning a team's members will feel they succeed or fail as a team and put pressure on one another without waiting for the leader's permission.

- You don't always need a Real Team. You only need one when group members can't reach the goal by working individually under a leader's direction. Thus, sometimes a Performance Group will be enough even under high-pressure conditions.

- The advantage of Performance Groups is that you needn't endure the trials of becoming a team. Developing into a team takes hard work, candour and usually some conflict, which can bruise egos. This may not be practical if you have key people who don't believe in the power of teams, won't share control or are difficult to work with ... and you can't replace or work around them.

- The advantage of Real Teams is that they'll always outperform Performance Groups if you set them up right and maintain them skilfully. They are better when you need major or urgent change in results and working practices, innovation, fast responses to competitors' moves or face creative or problem-solving projects.

- The key is to make a conscious choice between a Real Team and a Performance Group based on the challenge you and your colleagues are facing, the work you'll need to do and your attitudes to team disciplines.

- The Real Team versus Performance Group choice is not a one-time permanent decision. It's not what you are or need to be. It's what you are *acting as* or what you need to *act as*. Thus if you've mastered enough of the Real Team disciplines you can consciously flex your way of working according to the tasks you're facing and switch to Performance Group mode when it makes sense to do so.

6

Why So Few Senior Teams?

I'll remind you what I wrote near the start of chapter one:

> "Think of a few outstanding companies. Ask yourself, why are they exceptional? Perhaps you said it's because they're great at creating new products and services, disrupting old industries with a new business model, executing strategy, improving or delivering fabulous customer service, growing sales or cutting lead times. Whatever your answer, here's the common thread: beyond the start-up stage, their results didn't come from individuals working solo. They relied on people working together across disciplines to mesh their multiple skills and experiences.
>
> They prove that delivering superb results while standing out from competitors relies on combining human talents. And teams are the key to that – they are the building blocks to company-wide collaboration. Indeed, you could relabel 'team building' as 'the art of human collaboration'. Simply put, your ability to build and nurture teams decides whether you achieve consistent high performance across your department or business."

In my view, responsibility for creating a climate for across-the-board collaboration starts with the top people as they set the organisation's tone. They model the way for everyone. Now if you hold that thought while bearing in mind that CEOs and their top colleagues often grapple with issues of vision, employee engagement and organisational change – all challenges that suit real teams – you'd think senior teams would be common.

But as I remarked in chapter 4, few so-called senior management teams are real teams.[20] (By "senior" I mean at or near a firm's top executive tier.) This is not only my experience; it's supported by Katzenbach & Smith's research. So the question is: why are there so few genuine senior teams?

Top Performance Groups and Real Teams' Disciplines

In chapter 5 we uncovered the five basic differences in the ways Real Teams and Performance Groups work. But to explain why we see so few senior teams we'll have to zoom in closer on the working differences between top performance groups and teams.

Remember, they face different performance challenges. With Performance Groups, the sum of individual members' contributions is enough to deliver their main goal. But with Real Teams, their chief performance goal exceeds the sum of individuals' efforts. It's this difference in context that demands different disciplines.

In figure 10 you'll see 13 differences in the disciplines. We've already explained the five core contrasts in the previous chapter (numbers 1–5 greyed out). We'll run through those quickly before concentrating on the other eight.

Five core differences

In most senior performance groups you'll see single (sometimes dominant) leaders acting as the focal point of a hub-and-spokes model with little sharing of the leadership process. They'll usually preside over the group, rarely engaging in creative work with their colleagues.

NOTE: by "leadership process" I mean (1) ensuring there is an up-to-date **motivating purpose** while paying simultaneous attention to (2) the **task, progress and results** (3) **group**

unity and (4) **individuals' engagement**. I described this four-dimensional model in chapters 1 and 2 of my previous book, The Three Levels of Leadership (second edition).

However, in senior real teams, leaders share more of their power. They allow and encourage their colleagues to contribute to decision-making and co-determine how they should work together. Instead of imposing goals, they'll typically agree the team's aims with their colleagues unless the board has handed down a precise measurable goal (which would be unusual). Also, leaders of senior teams contribute to the task work; they don't stand on the sidelines.

Figure 10: Senior Real Teams vs Senior Performance Groups

Senior Performance Group	Senior Real Team
1. Dominant leader, less shared leadership	➡ One official leader, more shared leadership
2. Leader presides over the work of others	➡ Leader joins in and does real creative work
3. Members assigned to individual tasks	➡ Members work jointly on shared tasks
4. Individual work outputs determine results	➡ Collective work outputs determine results
5. Individual performance accountability (ethos: "only the individual can fail")	➡ Individual *and* joint performance accountability (ethos: only the team can fail")
6. *Broad purpose* delivered through others	➡ *Specific* performance goal *they* deliver
7. Measures its performance *indirectly* by its influence on others and via financial results	➡ Measures its performance *directly* by assessing their collective work outputs
8. High mutual respect but often *trust* gaps	➡ High mutual respect *and trust*
9. *Avoids* overt conflict	➡ *Encourages and handles* overt conflict well

Figure 10 continued...

Senior Performance Group	Senior Real Team
10. Stresses *efficient meetings that run on time* where they discuss, decide, share data and delegate, but do no collective creative or problem-solving work	➡ Encourages *open-ended discussions and creative problem-solving meetings* where they discuss, decide, share data, delegate and do creative / problem solving work together
11. *Individual ambitions are more important* than group purpose	➡ *Team purpose is at least as important* as individual ambitions and often more so
12. *Few members* have clear added-value roles when they meet as a group	➡ *All members* have clear added-value roles when working together as a team
13. *Stable roles and contributions* reflecting members' job titles, skills and talents	➡ *Shifting roles and contributions* reflecting the varying tasks and members' skills and talents

Inspired by and adapted from a table in *The Wisdom of Teams* by Katzenbach & Smith, 1993

Real senior team members spend more time together than their performance group equivalents. They have to because they deliver results through collective work – whether that's solving a problem, creating something new or jointly executing a plan. But members of senior performance groups, coordinated by the leader, largely work separately in their parts of the business. Why? Because that's enough to deliver their overall goal.

Behind the senior team's work outputs you'll see both individual and joint accountability, meaning the "performance pact" isn't only between leader and members. It's between members too. This creates helpful peer pressure, strengthening the ethos that "together we succeed or fail as a team". But in performance groups, leaders coordinate the members' work, ensuring only individual accountability, meaning the ethos is "only the individual can fail".

Eight other differences

A key contrast concerns purpose, goals and performance measurement (items 6 and 7 in figure 10). Real senior teams have performance goals specific and unique to them, goals they care about. Not only that, they know their #1 goal. It could be to create a new company vision or to transform the firm's culture or working practices. They measure success by asking whether they've achieved or are closing in on their goal. But senior performance groups won't always have a goal that's uniquely theirs. They'll typically have a broader purpose similar or even identical to their firm's aims – for example, "grow profits by 10%". They share this purpose with all employees and fulfil it by delegating work to people outside their group. The members will assess their success not by the difference they've made, which is hard to measure, but the company's overall results.

The eighth difference is the contrast in respect and trust. By "respect" I mean regard for another person's judgement and ability to make things happen. By "trust" I mean faith in another's motives – that we believe they mean what they say, that they have no hidden selfish agenda, that they'll do what they say they're going to do. In senior teams you'll find high trust *and* respect. However, in successful senior performance groups, although you'll find high mutual respect, the levels of trust in colleagues' motives won't match a team's.

How the group handles conflict marks the ninth difference. Senior teams don't duck conflict. They know it's an unavoidable – and often helpful – part of joint creative or problem-solving work and have the trust, attitude and collective skills to handle it well. But you'll find most senior performance groups shy away from conflict – especially overt conflict. It makes the members too uncomfortable.

Senior performance groups usually stress crisp agendas and well-run meetings that finish on time. How do they do it? By limiting their time to sharing and reviewing data, making decisions, and delegating work to others outside the group. Senior real teams do those too, but they also deliver creative collective outputs. For example, crafting a turnaround plan. This means they need more open-ended agendas. For them, finishing on time matters less than getting the job done. That's the tenth difference.

In teams, the overall goal is *at least* as important to members as their own ambitions, meaning they'll usually put the shared goals before their selfish aims. But you won't see this degree of self-sacrifice in senior performance groups as members' personal ambitions will usually trump the group's purpose if they have to choose between them. There's the eleventh difference.

The twelfth and thirteenth contrasts concern members' roles. In well-oiled senior teams all members know their roles and understand how they contribute to the team's cause. It means they feel included and valued. This is less common with senior performance groups because the members are often present only because they report to the senior executive. They're there by default. No one's asked, "What's our goal in getting together, what roles and skills are required, so who do we need here?" The result: you can see capable members who add value to the company but aren't essential to that group's purpose. They often wonder why they're present and feel bored ("this is wasting my time"). Or they don't feel fully included. Or they sense there's a "pecking order" and feel they're near the bottom. The other difference is that in senior performance groups the members usually adopt fixed roles reflecting their job titles. That's not so true in senior teams where roles often form and flex according to the agenda and members' strengths.

Overall, a senior team's motivation – its desire to achieve plus belief that it can succeed – and sense of unity is usually higher than a senior performance group's. Why? Four reasons. First, because teams agree stretching goals unique to them, goals they care about, which boosts motivation. Second, because they share decision-making about aims, means, priorities and ways of working. This takes their involvement and commitment up another notch. Third, because team members respect and trust one another and say what they need to say even if it means conflict. That removes hidden agendas and raises peer pressure to perform. Fourth, because all members have clear added-value team roles, making them feel included and important, raising motivation even further.[21]

Why So Few Senior Teams?

Those are the differences in working approach. Now we're ready to answer the question, "Why are there so few genuine teams at the top of companies?" Simply put, it's because senior executives find it hard to apply the thirteen team disciplines. Why? Because they face five blocks, which I'd summarise with this pyramid diagram:

Figure 11: Five Blocks to Senior Teams

No goal

Psychological risk

High egocentricity

Unexamined presuppositions

Ignorance of Pseudo, Real Teams & Performance Groups

Each block sets the foundation for the obstacle lying above it. At the pyramid's base is *ignorance*. Many executives don't know what a team's distinguishing features are and couldn't tell the difference between real teams and performance groups. Indeed, few know they have a choice of disciplines. Alternatively, they do know the difference but believe they face a one-time decision. They haven't realised you can switch disciplines according to the task. Just as important, they've never heard of pseudo teams. This narrowing of awareness sets the foundation for the problems you'll see one level higher in the pyramid.

At level two we meet senior people's five *unexamined presuppositions* about teams. I'm not saying all senior executives hold all five, but I am saying they're widely held in my experience. They are:

1. **"Teams don't work".** It stems from the ignorance I just described plus previous bad experiences in so-called teams. Dozens of executives down the years have told me about bickering, back-stabbing and boring, pointless, time-wasting meetings as they recounted their experiences in "teams". But in listening, it was clear they hadn't worked in real teams. They'd been in badly-run performance groups failing to apply the six basic disciplines you saw in the Y diagram (figure 9, chapter 5). Or, worse, they'd had the misfortune to spend time in a pseudo team. But they didn't know that.

2. **"Individual accountability trumps team accountability."** The idea that it's best to pin final responsibility on one person. But they don't realise this blocks the "we succeed as a team and fail as a team" mindset, which is crucial to team building. Unknowingly, that tilts them towards a performance group.

3. **"Job title and status should control people's influence around the table."** An unspoken idea that introduces feelings of superiority and inferiority, making it harder to form a real team. It's not universal, but it's common.

4. **"If you report to the CEO you're automatically in the team."** That's even if your mindsets, knowhow and skills won't improve (or could worsen) its results. This often undermines the unwritten team rule saying, "no passengers, everyone must add value".

5. **"People at the top aren't there to do real work."** I've noticed that many at senior level feel they've risen above the workspace and marketplace. They're not there, as they see it, to make products and services or deliver value to customers. They see their role as overseeing, delegating and criticising, not problem-solving, designing, creating and executing. They've lost the habit of doing real work when they meet. That, of course, goes directly against the purpose of real teams.

Can you see how the five presuppositions act as a sieve to make teams less likely and performance groups almost the default choice at senior level? But the story isn't over. When the five presuppositions join the blocks at levels 3 and 4 the chance of building a senior team shrinks further.

The third level is *high egocentricity*. Executives making it to the top are usually strong-willed and sometimes self-centred quirky individualists. They're usually good at what they do. But they're often laser-focused on their agenda, opinions and concerns because that's got them to where they are. All have been running departments, companies or divisions and, although you'll find exceptions, they're used to calling the shots. But in a real team they must collaborate with peers, which they can find tough if they're used to shaping the agenda. That sets them up for clashes or uncomfortable silent standoffs with colleagues of similar attitude and status... which takes us to the pyramid's next level.

At level four, being egocentric, they meet three forms of *psychological risk*. Remember, these people are used to getting their own way and doing things the way they want. They're unused to making commitments to colleagues, being open to peer review, having to face opposing arguments, being questioned by or receiving pressure from peers. Their bosses yes, but peers no. These are all features of joint accountability – a hallmark of real teams. But joint accountability poses three dangers because to egocentric executives it's not only unfamiliar, it's threatening. First, it could expose humiliating failures or mistakes. Second, it triggers the fear of losing autonomy and control. (Loss of freedom can worry them more than team results.) And third, there's the real danger of conflict because the chances of overt disputes are higher in teams than in performance groups. I've found most senior managers shy away from conflict. That can lead them to create an unspoken "I won't attack you if you don't attack me" pact. While it preserves their safety, it undermines joint accountability.

Finally, at the top of the pyramid, you'll often find there's *no overriding, stretching, team-specific performance goal*. The business can be facing huge challenges, but the top executives may not see a compelling performance-based goal demanding urgent collective action forcing them to act as a team. Now maybe they're right. Perhaps such a goal doesn't exist. But I've seen companies in crisis where senior executives can't see what's obvious to everyone else: that they face a clear specific performance challenge unique to them, a challenge they can only meet by acting as a team. What causes this blindness? It's partly senior executives' inclination to assume their purpose as a group is identical to the organisation's aims. But it's also the natural outcome of the pyramid's four lower layers. They don't ask themselves, "If this is the organisation's goal, what do *we* as a group have to deliver to make sure that goal is achieved?" Why would they look for goals that mean they run the risk of collaborating, doing problem solving, creative or executional work, giving up their "turf", holding one another accountable or running the unpleasant risk of conflict? They think, "Far better (that is, safer) to work as a performance group."

I'm not suggesting all senior groups need to act as real teams. For some, the performance group discipline makes more sense. But I do believe that if more top executives understood the difference between real teams and performance groups and grasped these five blocks – and used the kind of practical model I'll offer in Book Two of this trilogy to help them – we'll see more top teams. The payoff? I think you'll see higher employee engagement, higher customer satisfaction and better financial results.

The Key Points...

- Teams are the basic building blocks for achieving high performance across your organisation. If you want to be good at building and nurturing teams, start at the top because the senior people have their hands on the climate control dial. That's one reason why teams at the top should be more common. Another is that top executives are constantly wrestling with issues of vision, employee engagement and organisational change, which, as we saw in chapter 5, are all challenges suiting real teams.

- But teams at the top are not common, based on my experience and Katzenbach & Smith's research. Why not?

- The short answer to the "why" question is that top executives find it hard to apply the 13 disciplines of real senior teams.

- But that leads to another question: again why? I believe there are five blocks.

- One, ignorance. Many senior executives don't know the difference between teams and performance groups. That leads to a default choice for the latter. Few also realise you can switch disciplines according to your task, meaning your choice isn't permanent. Nor do they know the dangers of pseudo teams. This ignorance creates the foundations for the next four blocks.

- Two, unexamined presuppositions. There's the idea that "teams don't work", often because they've worked in pseudo teams without realising. Or the view that individual accountability trumps team accountability. Or that job title and status, not merit, should settle people's influence around the table. Or that if you report to the CEO you're automatically in the team. And, finally, that people at the top needn't do real work when they get together; they can simply delegate and criticise others' contributions.

- Three, high egocentricity. These are people who are used to calling the shots, not collaborating with peers of equal strength, ability and track record. This sets them up for unhelpful conflict or silent stand-offs, either of which make teams less likely.

- Four, psychological risk. There are three facets. First, autonomy. Many senior people fear losing autonomy and control because they like (and are used to) expressing their will freely. Second, joint accountability. I've met many top executives who feel uncomfortable being open to challenges from peers or promising teammates they'll complete tasks – teammates who could criticise them down the line. They'll accept such behaviour from bosses, but not peers. They're equally uncomfortable with publicly holding peers accountable, preferring to leave that to the leader. Third, conflict. It frightens them.

- Five, there's no stretching team-specific performance goal demanding collective effort. Partly because senior executives assume their purpose as a group is identical to the organisation's chief goal. But partly too because of the first four blocks.

- I think we'll see more high-performing companies when we have more real top teams.

- This doesn't mean I'm arguing that all top-tier work groups should act as teams. For those that focus on progress updates, information-sharing, decision-making, and delegating work to executives, like a company's board of directors, a performance group approach makes more sense. As I said in chapter 5, a performance group choice can often be valid.

7

Seeing Through the Fog I: Commit-Combust-Combine (Overview)

I had one big aim in introducing what I called the "dual forces" in chapter 3. It was to expose the numerous competing pressures in work groups to show it takes effort to become and stay a successful team. But while the dual forces story is good for explaining teams' psychological difficulties, it won't help you figure out what's going on amid the noise and confusion of team life, meaning it's not ideal as a diagnostic aid. So we'll correct that flaw in this and the next two chapters by helping you see through the fog. Not only that, we'll create the base for an analytical tool called TeamFixer®. I'll introduce it in Book Three.

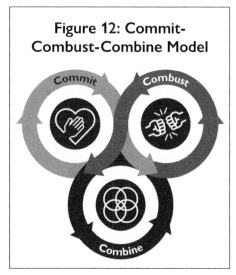

Figure 12: Commit-Combust-Combine Model

We'll start in this chapter by outlining the Commit-Combust-Combine model you see pictured in figure 12. Chapter 8 will explore its nuances in greater detail. And then chapter 9 will explain what can happen after Potential Teams reach Real Team status.

Roots of Commit-Combust-Combine

Since the late 1950s, researchers and thinkers have suggested theories to explain how groups and teams form and evolve.[22]

Bruce Tuckman's four stage "Form-Storm-Norm-Perform" model is the best known.[23] Tuckman felt the rhyming trick was its main claim to fame, but it taught a wider audience that groups often experience a "storming" (conflict and power struggle) phase. However, its usefulness is limited for three reasons. First, it describes *how* successful groups and teams evolve, but it lacks a psychological footing, meaning it doesn't explain *why* they evolve that way. That weakness makes it less helpful for understanding what's going on in the team while it's happening and figuring out what to do next. Second, it proposes a step-by-step sequence that rarely happens as cleanly and reliably in real life. Third, I question if it's useful to separate the "norm" and "perform" stages. In my view, they only complicate the model.

I've found William Schutz's FIRO (Fundamental Interpersonal Relations Orientation) research and theory more useful. He studied US naval teams at sea and first published his theory in 1958. He refined FIRO over the next 35 years, but it remained largely unknown to people in business. FIRO overcomes the three concerns I have about Tuckman's work. That's why I've used it as the jumping-off point in my thinking. Schutz deserves great credit because without his research there would be no Commit-Combust-Combine model.

The model I'm proposing builds on Schutz's theory by adding three changes to make it specific to performance groups and teams.[24] That means, unlike Schutz's theory, it doesn't try to explain social groups, therapy groups, training groups and volunteer-based task groups.

Link With Team Progression Curve

When you're in the thick of the action, the team building experience can feel confusing and volatile. Fortunately, Schutz's research revealed that if we dig below the behavioural chaos we can detect distinct issues controlling a team's formation or failure to form. These issues flow from basic psychological forces and whether members apply (or misapply) team disciplines. Understanding these issues and their underlying forces will help you in three ways:

- You'll make sense of what seem random behaviours, giving you a better idea of how to boosts the team's results.
- You're more likely to avoid the danger of becoming a Pseudo Team.
- It will boost your skill in applying the seven-principle (7P) model you'll meet in Book Two.

Figure 13: Team Progression Curve & C-C-C

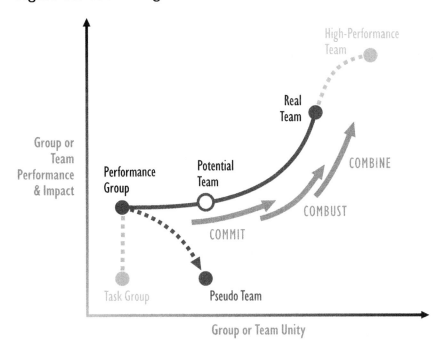

Figure 13 shows the Team Progression Curve I introduced in chapter 4. Underlying the ascent from Potential Team to Real Team and, occasionally, onward to High-Performance Team are the three growth issues I'm calling Commit, Combust and Combine (C-C-C). You see them shown as three curved arrows. The C-C-C model says all work groups face three issues that members must resolve to become and stay a successful team: Commit, Combust and Combine, usually (but not always) in that order. There's a point to stress here: the C-C-C model shows what *can* happen, but it doesn't imply that all work groups resolve their C-C-C issues enough to evolve from Potential Team to Real Team and then on to become High-Performance Teams. As I said in chapter 4, many Potential Teams get stuck and fail to deliver the results their companies need because they don't understand how to become and stay a team. And although Real Team is the natural next stage for a Potential Team if it puts in the right work, a High-Performance Team isn't the automatic next stage for a Real Team. As I explained in chapter 4, few Real Teams become High-Performance Teams.

In the next three sections I'll introduce the basics of Commit, Combust and Combine.

Commit

The central theme in Commit is *inclusion*. For each member it has two aspects: your inclusion (selection) of me and my inclusion (commitment) of myself.

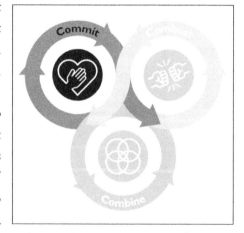

First, there's the decision on who to bring into the team to help it achieve its purpose. Second, there's the question of whether members' will act on their innate urge to connect, belong and take part in a shared task by dedicating themselves to the team's mission or instead remain aloof and uninterested.

You could boil down the Commit issue to two questions – one for the leader (or selectors) and one for each member:

> **Commit question #1:** What's our basic purpose … and therefore what blend of skills, knowhow and behavioural styles do we need … so who should we pick for this team?"

Commit question #2: Shall I be an active, engaged member and commit to this team or shall I stay detached, hold back, and remain on the sidelines?

We'll examine Commit's finer points in chapter 8, but we can say the team has resolved Commit – at least enough to move on to Combust – when it's met four criteria. One, the leader has chosen the members with the team's basic purpose in mind, meaning that although they may not be playing sharply defined roles yet, they each have distinct value-adding strengths. Two, the members understand the team's basic purpose and have agreed a number one goal they see as compelling, urgent and doable. Three, based on the role they sense they could play and their colleagues' behaviour towards them (notably the leader's), each member feels valued and included. Four, because of points 2 and 3, they've decided to play a full part, at least for now.

Combust

Combust centres on *power*. It flows from human beings' drive to achieve, to grow, to express their creativity and talents, control what's happening around them, be independent, take responsibility, and deliver a unique contribution. It shows as members' struggle to exert influence by playing valuable satisfying roles, which explains the turmoil and conflict you'll often see when Combust is at work.

For each team member, the issue revolves around five interwoven themes. One, our new team role's clarity and added value in our own and colleagues' eyes. Two, how much autonomy and, three, how much formal or informal responsibility that role brings us. Four, how much power we wield over the team's decisions. Five, how satisfied we are with our added value, autonomy, responsibility and power.

Although it's simplistic because it masks the nuances we'll examine in chapter 8, we could sum up each member's Combust issue with this question:

> **Combust question:** Am I seeking high or low influence, especially when we consider and act on team decisions, and will I face battles with my colleagues, so shall I act timidly, subtly or forcefully?

You can assume the team has largely resolved Combust when four power-related points are true. One, all members feel happy with their team roles and responsibilities. Two, they all understand and accept how the team decides the way forward. (For example, does the leader decide or does every member have a say? Is it majority voting? Is 100% agreement needed? Are mysterious "fait accompli" decisions taken behind closed doors? Is there an inner clique where certain members are more equal than others?) Three, they feel satisfied with their power to influence team decisions. Four, they feel a helpful team structure and sense of order has begun to emerge from the first three points.

Combine

Combine is more complex. It has two distinct but connected themes: *intimacy* and *focus*.

Intimacy takes us beyond our wish for mere contact (as in Commit) to want to feel closer to teammates, to support and be supported, to like and be liked. Intimacy, of course, demands trust. We build trust by being open – by saying what we really think, feel and intend – and doing what we promised colleagues we'd do.

Focus, the second theme, concerns where we direct our energy: in the team's interests or our own?

When intimacy and focus combine, they drive team members to support one another while expressing their individual potential in pursuit of the team's purpose, not their selfish interests. This is when you'll see joint accountability take hold, which creates a genuine team spirit. Now members hold themselves accountable for their efforts while insisting that colleagues play their parts. But you won't see scapegoating because their togetherness means the attitude is, "we succeed as a team or fail as a team." The fusion of intimacy and focus approaches its peak in a Real Team. It reaches its peak on the rare occasions you see a High-Performance Team.

We can capture the Combine issue in two questions:

> **Combine question #1:** Am I ready to trust the people here and say what I really think, feel, want and intend, even at the risk of making myself vulnerable … or shall I remain guarded?

> **Combine question #2:** Shall I put the team's priorities before my own interests and, if so, given what we need to achieve, how can I best use my talents to help us succeed … or shall I look after number one?

Although I'm simplifying, you can tell a team has navigated Combine successfully when you see four signs. One, the members regularly say what they are really thinking and feeling; in other words, they tell one another the truth – meaning no hidden agendas. Two, because of point one, they trust one another and have developed closer emotional bonds. Three, they always put the team's goals before their selfish interests. Four, they apply joint accountability, meaning they accept responsibility for their own parts in the team's results while holding their colleagues responsible for theirs, which includes confronting underperforming members without waiting for the leader's consent.

A Simple Summary

So far I've introduced the C-C-C model in only its most basic form. To be clear, it contains complications and intricacies. We'll delve into some of those here and the rest in chapter 8. But staying with its simplest form, we can summarise the model's three issues and associated questions in figure 14's "at-a-glance" summary table.

Figure 14: Commit-Combust-Combine Issues

Issue		Themes		Key Questions
Commit	➡	Inclusion	➡	Who's in? Engaged or uninvolved?
Combust	➡	Power	➡	My influence? Forceful, subtle or timid?
Combine	➡	Intimacy + Focus	➡	Open or guarded? "Me" or "we"?

Potential Teams climb towards Real Team status when they've done four things. One, they've defined their purpose and chief goal and realised it demands a team approach. Two, they've chosen their members wisely. Three, the members have addressed the C-C-C issues to their personal satisfaction. Four, they've put the team's goals ahead of their own.

By "addressed the C-C-C issues to their personal satisfaction", I mean they have *freely* chosen to respond the way they have, not adopted those behaviours to protect themselves from subconscious fears or because they feel intimidated by their colleagues. For example, if they stay quiet in team meetings, it's because they are genuinely comfortable with behaving that way in that moment. They don't feel colleagues have silenced them and – this is important – they could choose to speak up any time if they want to intervene.

Why the Commit-Combust-Combine Sequence?

Earlier, I said the Commit, Combust and Combine issues usually arise in that order. Why is Commit typically the first issue members face after they've joined the team? It's because if they don't answer the second Commit question with, "yes I'll engage" (at least for now), the team won't need to address the challenges of Power (Combust) and Intimacy-Focus (Combine). Again why? Because members won't care enough to worry about them. After all, Combust centres on influence. It will only come to the fore after members address their Commit needs because power and influence over the team are irrelevant if no one wants to stay or play a full part. The same is true of Combine, which is about intimacy, trust, collaboration and joint dedication to the mission. Why care if no one's committed?

Why does Combine normally follow Combust? Schutz found it's usually only after members gain enough feel for their power and position in the emerging team, through trial and error and by judging colleagues' reactions, that they turn to the Combine issue. That's when they show most interest in developing closer connections, building trust, supporting colleagues' needs, putting the team first, and seeking ways of raising collective performance. This makes sense because although you can quicken trust building (trust being the first of the two keys to Combine), members usually need time before they genuinely trust one another. Time, that is, for two things. One, repeated experiences of being safe to say what they're really thinking or feeling without being attacked or ridiculed. Two, repeated evidence that when colleagues say they're going to do something, they do it, and they do it well, meaning you can rely on them.

"Issues" not "Phases"

Here comes a key twist: although team members *usually* address Commit-Combust-Combine in that order, *they don't always*. So it's important not to see C-C-C as a three-stage version of Tuckman's four-phase model laced with a bit more psychology. As I've explained, there is a logic to the Commit-Combust-Combine sequence, which explains why they typically arise in that way, but they won't always appear in this order. Sometimes, for example, you'll see a Commit problem arise while the team is wrestling with Combust or both Commit and Combust difficulties arising during Combine.

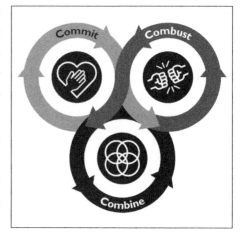

These are "micro issues". Micro issues are temporary relapses to an earlier issue while the Potential Team is climbing the curve.

That's why I depicted the model as the three-circle infinity loop you see here. Commit flows into Combust, which flows into Combine, but from there the team's energy can stay in Combine or slip back to Combust or even revert to Commit. And of course Combust may be followed by Commit if earlier unresolved Commit issues re-emerge before the team can shift to Combine.

This is because although at any moment only one challenge dominates the team's attention, all three issues remain below the surface – it's just that they're not equally obvious. What looks like resolution of one issue doesn't stop it reappearing in another guise (a micro issue) later. You can't, for example, address Commit and assume "it's all dealt with". Thus, the C-C-C model expects recycling of issues, meaning Committing, Combusting and Combining never ends.

I'll expand on micro issues and recycling in the next section so you'll get more detail there. The big point I want to make here is that C-C-C isn't a linear "phase model" like Form-Storm-Norm-Perform. Yes, the Commit-Combust-Combine sequence is broadly true and broadly matches the ascent from Potential to Real Team. But only broadly. You'll see exceptions. A team's formation and growth follows a complex path and although it's important to simplify it enough to create the diagnostic TeamFixer® tool I mentioned at the start of this chapter, it's equally important not to oversimplify. *My advice is to view Commit-Combust-Combine as three issues in the form of questions, not growth phases,* despite there being some truth to seeing them as sequential stages. Seeing them as issues rather than phases makes it easier to use them as diagnostic aids under pressure.

Micro Issues

To repeat, micro issues mark a previous issue's reappearance while the team is climbing the curve and grappling with a later issue. It's tempting to imagine a sequential story because if you could watch a Real Team from high altitude as it's forming, you'd see what appears to be the classic C-C-C sequence. But zoom in closer and you'd notice the micro issues in the form of mini loops. The picture in figure 15 shows what I mean.

Figure 15: Micro Phases in Combust and Combine

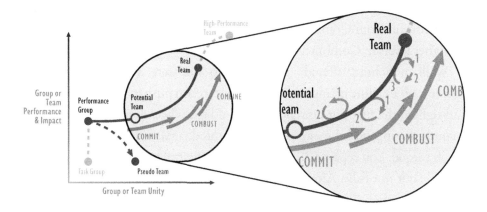

The mini loops show that although the team's trend is upward, it must sometimes repeat previous issues in shorter microbursts before continuing to climb the curve. Why do previous C-C-C issues reappear? There are two reasons:

- Few teams ever fully resolve the three issues. Yes, they resolve them enough to move onto the next challenge, but later, something will arise, causing them to revisit the previous issue. That "something" is what I call a "shift moment".

- Individual members don't address the C-C-C issues at the same speed. For example, an issue, perhaps Commit, can present such a deep psychological challenge for one member that it cuts across the main team issue, which may be Combust, complicating the picture.

Shift moments

Although you'll find one issue – either Commit, Combust or Combine – dominating the team's attention at any one moment, the other two remain latent because, to repeat, teams rarely fully resolve all three issues. Commit issues usually remain in Combust. Commit and Combust issues usually remain in Combine. And earlier Combine issues may resurface in Combine's more advanced stages.

The problem here is "unfinished business". You see, Commit ends as a main team issue when there's enough engagement to allow Combust to start, *not when the team has addressed all Commit-related challenges*. That's true of the transition from Combust to Combine. It also applies as the team climbs to higher levels in Combine.

William Schutz offered an analogy to illustrate a team's unfinished business.[25] Imagine fitting a wheel to your car. You push it onto the axle bolts and tighten the first nut just enough to hold the wheel in place. You attach a second nut opposite the one you just mounted, again without applying too much torque. You repeat with each opposing pair of nuts; you tighten them enough, but not fully. After completing the full set, you tighten the first nut a little more, then the others, again in opposing pairs. Finally, you tighten the nuts in a clockwise sequence to secure them.

You see a similar pattern in teams. Team members work on one issue until they resolve it enough to handle their task before turning their attention to the next C-C-C issue, but they'll return to the previous one for more "bolt tightening" later.

What prompts the further bolt-tightening? They face a "shift moment" that exposes the unfinished business. Here are five examples of shift moments:

- A new leader joins the team. (Or one or more other new members join.)
- The team faces an important task or challenge that's unfamiliar or controversial. Perhaps it reawakens Commit-related doubts around team purpose.
- Events in members' lives, like divorce or death, raise their sensitivity to C-C-C issues.
- An incident damages trust and confidence.
- One or more members find themselves locked in roles that don't suit their power needs and, after accepting them early on, they rebel against their restrictions, resulting in new Combust behaviour.

Whatever the exact cause, shift moments may require teams so do some brief recommitting, recombusting or recombining before returning to their task and continuing to climb the curve. This doesn't mean they have wasted their previous efforts as it's only a temporary relapse; just that they'll need to address the short-term setback before continuing their ascent.

Different speeds

As I'll explain in detail in chapter 8, team members' self-esteem problems affect the speed at which they resolve the C-C-C issues. Simply put, there's a direct link between Commit and your need to feel included, a similar correlation between Combust and how competent you feel, and a strong connection between Combine and doubts about your likeability. If you fear exclusion or being exposed as not good enough or you're afraid of rejection, you may rely on defensive behaviours to protect yourself, meaning it'll take you longer to resolve one or more of the C-C-C issues.

My point is that members usually address C-C-C issues at different speeds because their self-esteem problems vary. I'll explain with an example:

Imagine a five-member Potential Team with this mixture of self-esteem challenges:

Member 1: no serious self-esteem (SE) problems on any issue.

Member 2: deep SE problems in Commit and Combine.

Member 3: moderate SE problems in Commit and Combine.

Member 4: moderate SE problem in Combust and Combine.

Member 5: extra-deep SE problem with Combust, so much so that it cuts across whatever the team's main issue happens to be.

How might this play out? Three members (1, 4, 5) will feel comfortable moving quicker through Commit than members 2–3 who struggle with the first issue. When the main issue becomes Combust – because most members have resolved Commit enough to move on – members 2–3 may lag behind. After a delay, you may see the first micro issue (the reappearance of Commit) for those two members in the midst of Combust. Similarly, you may see Combust reappear as an issue in the middle of Combine because members 4–5 (especially member 5) are still struggling with problems around power and roles.

The message is that we're complex unique beings. We differ. Our needs around each C-C-C issue and what we actually receive from colleagues won't always coincide. This means team members react in different ways and at different speeds. For example, returning to the scenario I've just described, you could see four members starting to Combine once member 4 has dealt with his moderate self-esteem challenge around Combust, meaning it's now the dominant issue. But it's not the only issue in play as one – member 5 – is still Combusting due to her deep Combust-related self-esteem problem.

This points to another key insight: *although Commit, Combust and Combine are distinct issues, there aren't clean cut-offs between them.* Instead, there are fuzzy zones where one issue gradually fades until the next emerges.

To help you imagine the Commit-Combust-Combine process unfolding as the team ascends from Potential Team to Real Team while repeatedly cycling through the C-C-C micro issues, picture an upward spiral like the image you see in figure 16.

Figure 16: The Commit-Combust-Combine-Spiral

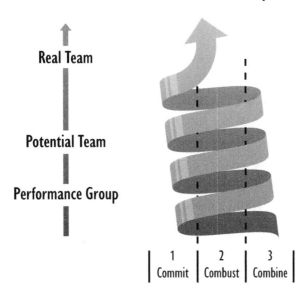

Real Team

Potential Team

Performance Group

| 1 | 2 | 3 |
| Commit | Combust | Combine |

Implications of Micro Issues

So what? What do micro issues mean in practice? Three things.

- First, they complicate the picture by layering one (micro) issue on to another (main) issue, making it harder to understand what's going on. But if members use the C-C-C model they'll find it easier to pinpoint the key problem while its happening and respond skilfully. So whenever the team is struggling, I recommend its members ask: which C-C-C issue is interfering with our performance and what do we do about it? I'll offer you the TeamFixer® tool in Book Three to support this questioning approach but to make best use of it, all team members should understand the C-C-C model underlying the tool.
- Second, individuals are individuals because they differ. It means the team must keep an eye on individual members' needs while working on team tasks. Naturally, one of the seven principles in Book Two's 7P action model addresses this point head on.

- Third, team leaders must recognise the occasional need for temporary backtracking when they notice one of the five shift moments has occurred.

How Long Does It Take?

Clients sometimes ask, "How long does it take to tackle the Commit, Combust and Combine issues?" I reply, "There's no fixed answer. It takes as long as it takes ... and sometimes the group never resolves them because its members lack awareness and knowhow"

I realise that answer is vague. Here's why. First, if you're coaching a work group through the C-C-C issues, you don't control the members' rate of progress, they do. What controls their rate of progress? The degree to which they open their minds, abandon any false ideas about teams and commit to practising new habits together, as elite sports teams would do. (This would also apply if the group was trying to climb the curve with no outside help.) Second, as I've explained, no work group ever fully resolves its C-C-C issues because it's a living system, meaning its members will change and new events will test its unity and productivity, throwing up new C-C-C challenges.

So I'll answer the question another way. You normally need to meet these conditions to be confident of addressing the C-C-C issues and reaching Real Team status:

Together you:

1. Have clarified your **motivating purpose**, meaning you have agreed:

   - your team's basic purpose, your raison d'être, your added value, making sure it aligns with how those above you in the hierarchy see it;
   - your number one goal for the next (maximum) twelve months, in writing, as a compelling theme with a supporting

scorecard showing 2–3 metrics and targets – a goal that motivates you all, that feels urgent to you all, that always remains in focus.

2. Have decided whether your number one goal needs you to apply a **Performance Group or Real Team** discipline.

3. Have grasped **how team leadership works**, meaning you:

   - have realised all Real Teams share leadership, that leadership is a four-dimensional process, not just one person's task (more on this in chapter 15);
   - feel the leader is addressing individual members' problem behaviours or attitudes.

4. Are addressing the often-ignored basics underlying success in **task progress and results**, meaning you:

   - have figured out which behavioural skills and technical knowhow you need, chosen team members on that basis and achieved a good people blend;
   - have ensured all members have clear roles they feel add value to the team's results, that give them the influence they want – roles their colleagues understand and appreciate, roles that make them feel included and valued;
   - have agreed explicitly how you'll make team decisions (vital for resolving Combust);
   - are consciously growing your collective skills in planning, creative thinking, problem-solving and decision-making;
   - have defined a vision of what you all want your department or company to become – or what you want your project to deliver – and why that's so great for those you serve – and backed it with a flexible, well-thought-out action blueprint;
   - are focusing on a few priorities at a time, avoiding the deadly mistake of doing too many things at once, which overloads

the agenda, scatters attention, retards progress and erodes group morale and unity. (And if you're a leadership group, you ensure you're not overloading everyone else's agenda and confusing your employees about their priorities);

- are applying the all-important discipline of joint accountability;
- are connecting and influencing skilfully with people outside the team while (if you're a leadership team) showing you're standing shoulder to shoulder and living the values you say you want to see in the organisation.

5. Are paying attention to the fundamentals of **group unity**, which in practice means you:

- have agreed an ethos and behavioural standards that define what's needed to be and stay a member of the team and how you'll work together … and you're applying it;
- trust one another's motives and believe that if colleagues say they'll do something, they'll do it … and from this have learned the habit of saying what you really think and feel, especially on sensitive issues;
- have learnt how to welcome and handle task-related conflict skilfully;
- are learning how to tackle the *content* (*what* you're discussing) while observing the *process* (*how* you're discussing it) and intervene when your conversational patterns begin failing you, as they will at times, which helps you name hidden elephants and stop avoiding useful conflict;
- have put the team's goals ahead of members' selfish interests'

6. Feel the team leader is **paying attention to individual members** as unique people, recognising what makes them tick and addressing their specific needs.

7. Are finding ways to keep **renewing** the team's upward progress, which includes:

- seeking new perspectives, new ideas or new members to avoid groupthink;
- pausing to learn and work on yourselves as a team;
- checking that you still believe your starting assumptions ... or updating them.

To be clear, these conditions represent a high bar. If your team meets them all, I'd say you've not only addressed your C-C-C issues, you're almost certainly an accomplished Real Team. You'll encounter these conditions and the same seven headings again when you read Book Two as they form the detail of that book's seven-principle (7P) action model.

Now if you asked, "How long does it take to address these conditions?", I'd reply that I don't think you'll resolve your team's C-C-C challenges in, say, a two-day off-site event. In my view, the timescale is anywhere between six months and infinity, depending on the would-be team's seniority. I say "infinity" because most senior groups never get anywhere close without help. They let years drift by, usually because they're unfamiliar with the psychological challenges they face, the disciplines to apply and the skills they need to learn. I say "depending on the work group's seniority" because I find most senior groups learn more slowly than junior teams. But you can never tell in advance as it depends how open-minded the team members are and whether they'll roll up their sleeves, learn the disciplines and practise new habits.

Skilled action by you and your team colleagues can of course quicken the pace. Explaining how to do so is this trilogy's main aim. You're more likely to accelerate your climb up the Team Progression Curve if you've grasped the C-C-C model's key messages. If you're a senior group *and* you and your colleagues put in the work *and* know what you are doing, I'd say you can become a Real Team within 12 months. If you work with a professional team coach, expect to hold 8–12 team coaching sessions in that time and perhaps a few more sessions after that where the coach intervenes in real-life meetings with agreed timeouts.

The Key Points...

- Chapter 3 had only one aim: to show the many pressures in work groups and stress that it takes effort to become and stay a real team, meaning they don't happen by accident. But that chapter's content isn't ideal as an analytical tool.

- This chapter's aim is – with chapters 8 and 9 – to prepare the ground for TeamFixer®, a tool you can use amid the noise and confusion of team life. I'll describe it in Book Three. The Commit-Combust-Combine model is one of the two foundations for TeamFixer.

- To become a Real Team, a Performance Group must navigate the three issues of Commit, Combust and Combine. Several pieces of research suggest you can't avoid these issues.[26] Your challenge is to speed up the journey, making it as smooth and surefooted as possible.

- This table sums up the heart of the Commit, Combust and Combine model:

Commit-Combust-Combine Issues Summary

Issue		Themes		Key Questions
Commit	➡	Inclusion	➡	Who's in? Engaged or uninvolved?
Combust	➡	Power	➡	My influence? Forceful, subtle or timid?
Combine	➡	Intimacy + Focus	➡	Open or guarded? "Me" or "we"?

- If you understand these issues and their underlying forces, it will help in three ways: (1) You'll make sense of what seem chaotic or random team behaviours, making it easier to figure out how to raise the team's performance. (2) You'll avoid the danger of becoming a Pseudo-Team. (3) It will boost your skill in applying the seven-principle (7P) action model you'll meet in Book Two.

- *Commit* centres on the two aspects of *inclusion*: who's selected and who chooses to include themselves psychologically. The first is the question of who should be picked for the team, given its purpose. The second is whether members will build on their innate urge to connect, take part in a shared task and belong to something greater than themselves, and commit to this particular team and its mission.

- *Combust* is about *power*. It flows from human beings' drive to achieve, to grow, to express their creativity and talents, control what's happening around them, be self-reliant, take responsibility and deliver a unique contribution. It shows as members' efforts to exert influence by playing roles that satisfy their power needs, which can involve fighting others. This explains the turmoil and conflict you'll often see when Combust is in force.

- *Combine* is more complex because you'll see two distinct but connected themes: *intimacy* and *focus*. Our desire for intimacy moves us beyond a wish for contact (in Commit) to want to feel closer to others, to like and be liked, to support and be supported. Intimacy requires trust. Building trust means we must say what we genuinely think, feel and intend, and do what we promised our colleagues we'd do. Focus concerns where we direct our willpower and energy: in the team's interests or our own? When we combine trust and focus, we support one another wholeheartedly while expressing our individual potential in service of the team's purpose, not our selfish interests.

- Commit is typically the first issue team members face. Why? Because if they don't decide to engage (at least for now), the team won't need to address the Combust and Combine challenges. Again why? Because members won't care enough to worry about them. Why would they care if no one's committed?

- Why does Combine normally follow Combust? Because research shows it's usually only after members gain enough feel for their power and position in the emerging team that they turn to the Combine issue. That's when they show most interest in developing closer connections, building trust, supporting colleagues' needs, putting the team first, and seeking ways of raising collective performance.

- Although Commit, Combust and Combine usually arise in that order, they don't always because of micro issues. Micro issues mean Commit issues can arise during Combust and both Commit and Combust issues can arise in Combine. That's why I depicted the  model as a three-circle infinity loop. Commit flows into Combust, which flows into Combine, but from there the team's energy can stay in Combine or slip back to Combust or even revert to Commit. And of course Combust may be followed by Commit if earlier unresolved Commit issues re-emerge before the team can shift to Combine. This is why I recommend you view Commit, Combust and Combine as issues, not sequential phases.

- For this same reason, although the Commit, Combust and Combine issues are distinct, you won't see clean, crisp cut-offs between them. They overlap and blur into one another.

- Micro issues have two causes: (1) "shift moments", which expose the reality that teams never fully resolve the three issues; (2) individual members addressing the C-C-C issues at different speeds because of their varying self-esteem problems.

- Micro issues have three practical implications for leaders and team members. One, they confuse the picture, making it harder to understand what's going on. This is why the C-C-C model is helpful in seeing through the fog. Two, they highlight the importance of watching out for members' differing speeds around the C-C-C issues. Three, occasional temporary C-C-C backtracking will be necessary, meaning you shouldn't see it as bad news.

- How do you know when your team has resolved the C-C-C issues? We'll examine this in more detail in the next chapter, but for now we can say:

  - It has resolved Commit – at least enough to move on to Combust – when it's met four criteria. One, the leader has chosen the members with the team's basic purpose in mind, meaning each have distinct value-adding strengths, even though they may not yet be playing sharply defined roles. Two, the members understand the team's basic purpose and have agreed a number one goal they see as compelling, urgent and doable. Three, based on the role they sense they could play and their colleagues' behaviour towards them (notably the leader's), each member feels valued and included. Four, because of the second and third points, they've decided to play a full part, at least for now.

  - The team has largely resolved Combust when four power-related points are true. One, all members feel happy with their team roles and responsibilities. Two, they all understand and accept how the team reaches decisions. Three, they feel satisfied with their power to influence those decisions. Four, they feel a helpful team structure and sense of order has begun to emerge from the first three points.

- You can tell a team has navigated Combine successfully when you see four signs. One, the members regularly say what they're really thinking and feeling. They tell one another the truth, meaning no hidden agendas. Two, because of point one, they trust one another and have developed closer emotional bonds. Three, they always put the team's goals before their selfish interests. Four, they apply joint accountability, meaning they accept responsibility for their own parts in the team's results while holding their colleagues responsible for theirs, which leads to peer pressure, and may include members confronting underperforming teammates without waiting for the leader's consent.

• There's no firm answer to the question of how long it takes to address the C-C-C issues enough to become a Real Team. There are certain conditions to fulfil, which I've grouped under seven headings. You'll meet them again in Book Two as they represent the seven principles of that book's action model. One thing you can be sure of: you won't address all your C-C-C issues in one off-site event. You'll almost certainly have to work on it over several months.

8

Seeing Through the Fog II: Commit-Combust-Combine (Detail)

This chapter builds on chapter 7's overview to deepen your grasp of the Commit-Combust-Combine model, allowing you to recognise the C-C-C issues as they're playing out. As we examine each C-C-C issue in detail to understand their nuances and complications, we'll apply these same ten subheadings:

- Team purpose and goal
- Team composition
- Members' early questions
- Individual members' focus
- Relationships and roles
- Members' typical behaviour
- Members' behavioural preferences
- Members' self-esteem complications
- Problems to watch out for
- Resolution of issue

This will make the descriptions in the next three sections easier to follow and compare.

Commit: A More Detailed View

The Commit issue starts when people are being considered for selection and unfolds as new members meet and figure out how much they want to engage.

Team purpose and goal

A team's basic purpose – its reason for being – is usually set just before Commit starts, but you'll often find it's fuzzy. So teams need to sharpen their purpose and make it motivating by expressing it as a number one goal for a specific period, backed by metrics and targets.

> **Note**: a team's basic purpose and its number one goal are keys to navigating the Commit issue successfully, but they don't stop being important when Commit ends. They remain huge influences over a team's climb up the Team Performance Curve throughout the Commit-Combust-Combine journey. Getting the basic purpose and number one goal right is crucial.

A team's basic purpose will guide selectors in picking members, the first part of Commit. But its shorter-term more measurable form – the number one goal – is central to achieving the second part: getting new members to engage fully. They must care about the goal. It must feel urgent and important to them. How much they care partly depends on their feelings about the team's challenge, whether the goal coincides with their personal values (the beliefs that guide and motivate them), and partly on whether they believe they can achieve it. If team members see the goal as worthwhile, exciting and doable, they'll want to stick around. They'll tell themselves, "This goal motivates me, I want to be part of achieving it." Now the budding team has a good chance of resolving Commit, at least enough to move on to Combust. The opposite will of course be true: an uninspiring goal will mean it can't unite and galvanise the members, making it less likely it'll resolve Commit successfully.

My point is that defining a compelling goal to unite and energise the team at the start is a "must" if it is to address the Commit issue. However, as I said in chapter 4, the goal must present a big enough challenge to make members combine their skills, knowhow and experience to deliver results they couldn't achieve apart. Otherwise you don't need a team – a Performance Group would be enough.

Team composition

Team leaders or selection panels usually decide who joins the work group. Ideally, they choose members after posing the first Commit question: *"What's our basic purpose ... therefore what blend of skills, knowhow and behavioural styles do we need ... so who should we pick for this team?"*

I say "ideally" because I find selection for senior teams doesn't get the thought it deserves. Yes, leaders will choose members for their technical, department or regional knowhow, but they usually ignore the need to craft a winning blend of behavioural styles – a blend that'll help those members click when they start working together. Real Teams achieve this blend by having all members play distinct added-value roles, roles their teammates understand and appreciate. Because the roles are distinct, they demand specific mindsets and behavioural strengths. That's why it's so important to ask if your team has the blend of mindsets and behavioural skills it needs and, just as important, if it's allowing its members to use their strengths to best effect when they work together.

The need to build a successful blend of behavioural mindsets and skills is obvious in elite sports teams – after all, what top football team would want eleven goalkeepers or eleven Diego Maradonas ... one yes, but eleven? However, it's not so obvious in industry. In the business world, we assume we have the right blend if we appoint the heads of Sales, Manufacturing, Finance, R&D, IT and HR, or perhaps regions or business units to the top team. But job titles – reflecting technical knowhow and experience in one part of the business – don't guarantee the right behavioural blend. So what does?

The answer is *diversity*. Not diversity of gender, race, social class or sexuality, but diversity of belief, thought and behaviour. This is where we turn to Meredith Belbin's research into executive teams.[27] He uncovered nine behaviour clusters (he called them team roles) that all business work groups need in their ranks to succeed. These behaviour clusters largely flow from members' values, intellects, talents, skills and life experiences, but the company's culture can also influence which team roles they play. In Book Two (chapter 16) we'll discuss Belbin's research and how to use it in more detail, but to explain what I mean by team roles, here are short sketches of Belbin's nine "behaviour clusters", using his labels:

- **Plants:** Propose ideas and suggestions for solving complex problems. Challenge unspoken assumptions. Create original solutions. Invent new ways of tackling issues. Look at subjects from a different angle and ask questions that unlock fresh insights. Conceive new answers.
- **Shapers:** Inject energy and urgency into the team. Get things moving. Stop complacency and laziness. Make sure the team is achieving its goals and doesn't duck issues. Push the team to move beyond obstacles.
- **Implementers:** Get down to practical issues. Push to turn ideas into pragmatic next steps. Nudge the team to agree clear action choices on what they will and won't do. Make sure the team has solid plans and processes with metrics, deadlines and clear responsibilities.
- **Teamworkers:** Boost the "emotional glue" between team members by reacting to their needs. Mediate and defuse angry confrontations. Use their popularity to win support for ideas. Encourage members who need their morale boosting.
- **Coordinators:** Help others work towards common goals. Keep the team's eye on the big picture. Clarify the team's purpose and goals. Promote decision-making. Ensure the team's tasks are delegated. Match individual talents to the team's aims and challenges.
- **Resource Investigators:** Connect the team with the outside world, e.g. fellow employees, customers, suppliers, advisers, investors and regulators. Ensure the team explores new opportunities and develops new contacts. Help the team solve problems by finding outside resources.
- **Monitor Evaluators:** Act as the critical counterpoint to rash judgements and dangerous rushes of blood. Ask the crucial, tough, sober questions about risks and what could go wrong. Ensure aims are wise, plans are solid, and use of time and money is sensible.
- **Completer Finishers:** Ensure high standards of execution. Insist on high quality and push for on-time delivery. Stress

rigorous follow-through and attention to detail by looking for errors, omissions and inconsistencies. Make certain the team doesn't leave issues "hanging".

- **Specialists:** Bring technical knowhow in specialised subjects relevant to the team's aims and field of work. Provide the team with deep expertise in narrow but important fields.

One important note: this doesn't mean all teams need nine members as many of us can play two Belbin team roles comfortably. Sometimes three.

Here's the big point: if you're missing key behaviour clusters (team roles) or have too many members with similar behaviour profiles, it will aggravate all three C-C-C issues, starting with Commit, making your group less likely to climb the Team Progression Curve. For example, you will find members clashing (or behaving passive-aggressively) and failing to agree. Or struggling to solve problems and deliver creative solutions. Or coming up with ill-considered plans. Or executing sloppily. Or launching time-wasting leadership coups. In short, if teams lack a good behavioural blend, they're unlikely to solve problems, plan well and make things happen.

We'll return to this subject in chapter 16 but the point for now is that teams need a blend of behavioural styles and mindsets to navigate C-C-C successfully, especially Commit. If you focus on job titles and put together a mix of departments or regions or business units you're unlikely to get the mix you want. The trouble is, few Potential Teams consider the behavioural blend question because most people don't know about Belbin's research into team roles.

Members' early questions

Once they're chosen to join the team, members will have private unspoken questions. In chapter 7, I summarised the second basic Commit question as: *"Shall I be an active fully engaged member and commit to this team or shall I stay detached, hold back, and remain on the sidelines?"* Note that it's not as simple as, "Am I in or out?" That's because in performance groups and real teams, especially leadership or professional sports teams, we often have little choice on whether to join as it goes with the job. However, we can be physically present without being mentally and emotionally engaged, meaning we can choose how much we genuinely commit ourselves.

Although the basic question I just posed expresses the nub of the issue, it hides important nuances, so let's reveal the finer detail. The first questions members usually (subconsciously) ask themselves in Commit are:

- What's our team's aim and do I really want to contribute to achieving it?
- Do I feel comfortable in this team; do I feel I belong here?
- Who responds favourably to me or sees things the way I do (or appears to)?
- What will the leader be like?
- Will they (especially the leader) accept me?
- Will they think I can make a difference to our results? Do I think I can?
- Will they ignore or dismiss what I say?
- Will it be a successful team?

Individual members' focus

When the Commit issue dominates, team members direct their energies inward so they aren't fully available for team performance. They may appear to attend to the task but their real focus is on personal safety. Think of Commit as a period of orientation, partly to the task, but mainly to one's team colleagues. Members will often worry about their degree of emotional comfort and what their colleagues think and feel about them and, notably, where they stand in the leader's eyes. This leads them to wonder what it's right to do and say – or not do and say – during team get-togethers. Members will therefore test what behaviours the team will accept, judging by their colleagues' responses and especially the leader's reactions.

Relationships and roles

In parallel, they begin searching for a satisfying role although this will
continue into Combust. Throughout Commit each member is – to varying
degrees – emotionally dependent on others' responses to them, especially
the leader's. They'll often feel vulnerable. That's why their behaviour may be
guarded. Relationships are usually superficial at this point. The members get
work done but performance is well below potential.

Members' typical behaviour

When Commit is in play, you'll often hear superficial conversations about
mutual acquaintances, the weather, what people did at the weekend and
so on. These chats serve a purpose: they allow members to learn about one
another. They discover answers to questions like: Who responds favourably
to me here? Who seems to share my opinions? How does the leader react to
me? Do I feel I belong here? What role might I play in this team?

Members' behavioural preferences

While wrestling with these questions, team members' natural behavioural
preferences around meeting new people and working in groups will influence
their approach to Commit.

Members who strongly prefer working alone or with people they already
know and trust will be slower to commit to the new team. Those who enjoy
working in new groups will usually be keener to join in. How quickly they
do so will depend on whether they prefer starting conversations with new
people or whether they want others to make the first move by doing something to include them. Yet others, who are somewhere in the middle, may be
cautious at first, but readier than the first group to commit.

These differing attitudes to Commit make it harder for members to
interpret their colleagues' behaviour and figure out where they stand.

However, team members always find a way of answering the eight Commit questions listed on page 124 – accurately or inaccurately – so if you don't allow this learning in team sessions, it will happen outside them or at unhelpful moments. For example, members may use the first decision-making moment to deal with unresolved Commit issues. This can slow decision-making or damage the decision quality if members' personal fears colour their thinking, especially if they're gripped by self-esteem issues, which we'll look at next.

Notes on natural behavioural preferences:

1. "Natural" means behaviours reflecting our true strengths, not our fear-based defensive habits.

2. By "preferences", I mean, for example, whether members prefer to engage in team tasks or would rather work solo (which affects Commit); whether they'd rather take charge or receive orders and opt for a quieter life (which influences what happens in Combust); and whether they enjoy forming close relationships or prefer to stay at arm's length (which will affect Combine).

3. People's natural behavioural preferences in groups and teams aren't fixed. You may, for example, place a higher value on working alone than a fellow team member, but there'll be times when you choose to be with others. And you may prefer positions of responsibility with power over others, but there could be times when you choose to take a back seat and accept their influence over you. The point is, when your behaviour is natural, *you are choosing your behaviour, you are being "you", you aren't a slave to your fears of being ignored, humiliated or rejected.*

4. This same principle will apply when we discuss members' typical natural behaviour in Combust and Combine.

Members' self-esteem complications

I introduced the power of self-esteem issues in describing the Individual forces (notably self-image beliefs) in chapter 3's Dual Forces model. The key point is this: self-esteem issues interfere with team members' natural behavioural preferences. *This is true for all three C-C-C issues.*

Self-esteem issues arise in Commit if members hold subconscious doubts about their innate significance and worthiness to be in the team. This is when they hold beliefs like, "No one's interested in my opinions here" or "I'm inferior to these people" or "I have no place here" or "They won't think I can add value to this team." In my experience, it's common for able experienced people to feel inferior or worry about their status without understanding why. This causes Commit's number one fear: the experience of being ignored or dismissed by colleagues. You may think this fear is rare, but I assure you it is not, even among senior executives.

Members holding these beliefs will work hard to avoid this fear. Keeping things simple, imagine a bipolar scale, like the picture below, with two opposite responses.

Defences Against Being Ignored or Dismissed

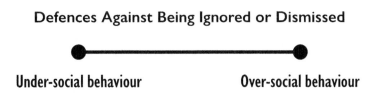

Under-social behaviour   **Over-social behaviour**

At one end is "under-social behaviour". At the other end, "over-social behaviour".[28] *Yet both behavioural polarities are subconscious means of defending against the same underlying status-based fear of being ignored or dismissed.* The key is understanding that both behaviours will emerge without conscious choice on members' part. Unlike natural behavioural preferences, the members aren't choosing their responses. It's as though they're being driven by internal fear-based computer programs.

In my experience with executives, under-social behaviour is common. This can show as members being repeatedly late for meetings or declaring on arrival that they "can't stay long" or claiming they have several conflicting duties, causing absence. During meetings you may see them showing scant interest in the team's task, instead perhaps staring at their smartphones. Or they may appear withdrawn. Or you may see them keeping a low profile by saying little even though they do have something to say and, indeed, would like to say it, but don't.

Over-social behaviour isn't rare, but I've found it's not as common at senior level as under-social conduct. You'll notice a cruder version when members try too hard to be visible, perhaps by being loud or ultra-gregarious, forcing others to notice them. Subtler versions include trying to be popular and instantly likeable or attempting to impress by name-dropping or seeking to adopt high-status mannerisms to look powerful. Over-social behaviour can appear helpful, but it doesn't represent commitment any more than its opposite. It's superficial play-acting.

My point is that self-esteem problems around self-significance will trigger various unhelpful responses to the Commit question of engagement, making this team issue harder to resolve.

Members with few doubts about their innate significance – who don't fear being ignored or dismissed – will find Commit easier to handle. Their lack of fear means defensive reactions won't blindly lead them. Although how much they prefer being included or excluded in new teams will vary, they'll usually respond to Commit in a more flexible, balanced manner because they can choose their emotional and behavioural responses to life in the new team.

Problems to watch out for

You will often see these behaviours when teams begin and while the Commit issue is alive, but they become genuine problems when they persist:

- Superficial conversations (or, alternatively "all talk and no action").
- Members not paying attention.
- Members withdrawing or wanting to withdraw.
- Repeated lateness or absence.
- Members' body language suggesting they feel excluded.

- Members not speaking up even if they have a different opinion or perspective.
- Pairing up (mini cliques) and colluding for self-protection.

Resolution of issue

Although I'm simplifying a complex process, we can say your team has resolved Commit sufficiently when you've appointed the members you think you need (given the blend of skills, knowhow, behavioural styles and mindsets you wanted) and most members have made the minimum commitment needed for the emerging team to move on to the next issue. This means:

- They believe the team's aim is sufficiently worthwhile and realistic.
- They have assessed their colleagues' reactions to them and feel included.
- They can at least sense a value-adding role for themselves.
- Stemming from the first three points, they've decided they want to stay and play their part in the would-be team ... at least for now.

As I noted in chapter 7 when writing about recycling of issues, you'll see degrees of commitment. In Commit, we're talking about the minimum dedication needed to take part. Commitment levels can – and do in successful teams – rise as they climb the progression curve, which is why Committing isn't a one-time event. It's a cumulative-cyclical pathway. That's partly why the team progression curve on page 97 shows the three issues overlapping.

Combust: A More Detailed View

Once enough members decide "they're in", meaning the team's aim matters to them, they feel reasonably included and understand when it's safe to speak up, Combust can begin. But not until then. Why? Because Combust issues are irrelevant if members don't take their inclusion in the would-be team seriously.

Combust centres on members' efforts to assert themselves as they carve out roles, set targets, solve problems and reach decisions while carrying out their part of the team's task. Their challenge is to satisfy three drives. One, their varying needs for power, whether that's influence or control. Two, their need to find a rewarding role and feel they can win their colleagues' respect by making a difference. Three, their need to create a sense of order.

This issue *must* arise if a real team is to emerge. Why? Because members have to learn how they're going to make decisions, which roles each person will take in reaching them, who holds what power and who does what when it comes to delivery. In this way, they gain a sense of order and structure. So Combusting is a good sign; it shows the Potential Team is starting to climb the Team Progression Curve.

Team purpose and goals

If the team's purpose is already clear and members have breathed life into it by defining a measurable common motivating goal, the conditions for Combust are favourable. Remember, "motivating" means a goal all members want to achieve *and* believe they can deliver. A common motivating goal helps "oil the wheels" by unifying the members and providing an emotional glue to offset their selfish interests and fears as they grapple with power issues. However, if the team lacks a clear motivating goal, Combust can't happen. The team will still be wrestling with Commit.

Team composition

In Combust, teams don't usually question if they have the right people on board. Why? Partly because they should have chosen their people well enough in Commit to start work and move on to Combust. But also because the members are too focused on finding satisfying roles. You're more likely to see a composition question reappear in Combine.

However, if it does arise in Combust, it's because members see a skill or knowhow gap that's so obvious they know they must plug it, or it's because they're at one another's throats or aren't getting much done. From experience, I would say the last two problems suggest they're missing one or more Belbin roles.

Members' early questions

On page 100 I summarised team members' main Combust question like this: *"Am I seeking high or low influence, especially when we consider and act on team decisions, and will I face battles with my colleagues, so shall I act timidly, subtly or forcefully??"* My intent was to capture the issue's essence, but it hides important subtleties we need to surface. Members will ask themselves these questions – again, usually subconsciously – when Combust issues are forefront in the team's growth story:

- What do I want to achieve in this group?
- How do we get things done here and what's my part in it, what's my role?
- Am I happy with that role?
- Will I be good enough? Can I cope?
- Who are the most powerful people here?
- How much power do I want and what kind – obvious formal responsibility or behind-the-scenes influence?
- What are the rules here?
- Can I make, change or break the rules?
- Am I ready to limit my autonomy by letting others influence and challenge me?
- Do I need to fight anyone here?

Not surprisingly, these questions can lead to struggle, which may outplay as overt conflict. Many people dislike or shun conflict so Combust can be an uncomfortable experience. Yet if members don't agree the roles they're going to play and learn how to solve problems, reach decisions and plan together, the Potential Team can't become a Real Team.

Individual members' focus

In general, as in Commit, members direct their energy inwards towards personal goals. Unfortunately, that's often unhelpful. In Commit, they wrestled with questions of prominence, visibility, prestige and status, but Combust concerns power, or rather their power needs, which will vary. They'll try to carve out satisfying roles while feeling comfortable with their control over team decisions and their impact on its results. This means balancing their urge to directly influence or even control their teammates and team results (high power needs) versus their desire to sit back, let their colleagues take responsibility and follow orders (low power needs).

Relationships and roles

Combust is like Tuckman's "Storm" phase. Members strive to assert enough independence by making their views heard while trying to find and play a satisfying team role, which can lead to misunderstandings and conflict. Simultaneously, they also wrestle with how much autonomy they are willing to sacrifice as they work on team tasks, which can be hard for members who value their independence.

Combust is therefore more about settling into your team position around problem-solving, planning, decision-making and execution than true cooperation. Yes, as we saw in Commit, work will get done, but performance and results will remain far below Real Team level because members' are directing their energy towards resolving the Combust issue to their personal satisfaction, not wholehearted collaboration.

Members' typical behaviour

You'll see a wide behavioural range when Combust is in force. Silence, disputes, sulking, dominating behaviours, rebellion, submission, blind obedience and shallow collaboration may be on show in what is, at heart, a power struggle. An external power struggle with colleagues, sure. But also internally as members strive to find the high-versus-low power balance that suits them best in *this* team with *these* specific colleagues. You see, members can display different power needs and behaviours in different teams.

Members' behavioural preferences

One reason you'll see a wide range of behaviours is that people's natural preferences towards power vary. This builds on the earlier point about power needs. Some members like dominating and taking charge. Others want to be less visible and influence from a back-seat position, playing the "power behind the throne" role. Yet others would rather have less responsibility and let colleagues tell them what to do ("faithful lieutenant" roles). And others may prefer playing "nonconformist thinker". These differences mean it's harder for team members to read one another, making it tougher to resolve Combust.

Another reason for the wide range is that, once more, self-esteem issues arise, which only complicates team life further.

Members' self-esteem complications

Members's self-esteem – as in Commit – will influence how they handle the ten questions on page 131. A self-esteem deficit will distort their natural behavioural preferences. It does so by taking away their choice, meaning they can no longer control or flex their behaviour at will. Instead fear is driving them, causing them to behave defensively, repeatedly, in ways that don't help the team.

Whereas the Commit self-esteem problem concerned feelings of *significance*, in Combust it's about feelings of *competence*. If, subconsciously, the member's self-image leans towards inadequacy, of "not being good enough", of feeling unable to cope, of being an impostor who'll be found out, he or she'll feel exposed to the risk of public failure. For them, the idea of making mistakes, not delivering or not knowing the answers is terrifying because it raises the fear of humiliation. They'll do almost anything to prevent themselves experiencing humiliation, or rather, the risk of humiliation.

Again, you may feel the "not good enough" belief and fear of humiliation must be rare, but it's not. I've found it's almost universal among senior successful people in every culture.

As in Commit, members holding these beliefs and their associated fears of public failure, mistakes and humiliation, will outplay them in their behaviour. As before we can draw a simple bipolar scale to show the typical behavioural responses:

Defences Against Being Humiliated by Failure or Mistakes

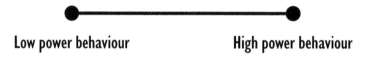

Low power behaviour   **High power behaviour**

Low-power behaviour is about avoiding roles and decisions involving influence, responsibility and control even when it makes sense to take a leading role because you have, say, more experience than your colleagues or superior technical knowhow. Members responding to their fear in a low-power way may act submissively, assume more junior positions in the team and prefer others to tell them what to do because they can blame them if things go wrong. This can cause serious trouble when the person playing this game is the official leader. People like this won't do what's needed to correct parts of the team that aren't working. They will delay or procrastinate or get caught in analysis-paralysis, seek perfect answers or avoid decisions by trying to "kick the can down the road". The buck won't stop with them.

High-power behaviour focuses on dominating and controlling colleagues or competing with them even when it's unhelpful to the team. This may show as an obvious dictatorial style, especially on the leader's part, perhaps supported by intellectual superiority or political connections or by endlessly criticising members to put them down. It can also show more subtly in the leader and other members as seductive behaviour (making promises that appeal to individual members' needs or vanity) or misleading them (hoping not to be exposed later). Another subtler high-power method you'll see is team members playing their cards close to their chest for fear of losing influence or, worse, being exposed as inept at leadership.

The key is to grasp that *both polarities are ways of dealing with members' limiting beliefs and deep fears about their competence deficits.* One way seeks to avoid the issue by ducking responsibility. The other seeks to assuage it by taking charge and trying to prove your competence repeatedly while stopping others from showing you up. Both represent subconscious, coping patterns of behaviour that lock team members into unhelpful habits, making Combust harder to resolve.

Some team members (not many in my experience) will harbour zero doubts about their innate ability to assert themselves, project power, influence others and contribute to the team's success. They feel good about their ability. The more they feel this way, the more they'll feel comfortable taking charge *and* accepting orders where needed. Their behaviour won't be fuelled by fear. They'll be ready to take on tasks or challenges and believe colleagues will trust their advice, decisions and ability to execute. Their natural preferences around power (that is, exerting power versus being happy to accept others' orders) will influence how they act in Combust, but they can vary their behaviour at will as needed.

Problems to watch out for

Every would-be team must navigate the Combust issue so the behaviours you'll see in Combust aren't automatically "bad". They are so common it's best to expect them. However, they turn into real problems if they persist. Look out for:

- Members competing to act as overall leader.
- Over-long discussions on how to approach a task.
- Aggressive, dominant members who intimidate colleagues.
- Submissive members who pretend to agree but don't really.
- Awkward passive-aggressive silences.
- Blaming and scapegoating.
- Cliques competing against one another.
- More powerful members presenting "fait accompli" decisions (decisions taken off-line in private) to colleagues.
- Anger and accusations.

- Overt rebellion.
- An obvious dip in commitment to the original team goal.
- Non-existent follow-through or chaotic or sloppy execution of so-called decisions.

Resolution of issue

Throughout Combust, members will wrestle with the ten questions listed on page 131 and the difficulties caused by their self-esteem issues. The shift to Combine begins when:

- Members settle into satisfying team roles.
- They understand and accept how the team reaches decisions... and act on them.
- They know who plays what role in those decisions.
- Most (ideally all) members are satisfied with their own power and influence in the team.
- A sense of order, structure and progress emerges from points one, two, three and four.

This does, of course, assume the members still believe in their common motivating purpose and want to remain engaged in the team.

Combine: A More Detailed View

In Combine, our urge to be liked, to get close to others, to build trust and to support one another coexists with our drive for achievement and personal growth. If members resolve this issue, they open up, learn to trust one another, build stronger emotional bonds and recognise how much they need each other's knowhow, skills and contacts. At the same time – and this is crucial – they put the team purpose ahead of their personal aims. The team's purpose becomes their focus. When this happens, you have a willpower-affection fusion. This is the signature feature and high point of Combine. The result? Team performance leaps forward.

Unfortunately, Combine is a complex team issue. It needs members to balance *personal needs* and *team needs*, meaning they're trying to deepen their personal connections while strengthening attention to collective performance. It's not one or the other. It's both. This makes it a tough challenge, but this dual focus is the key to resolving the Combine issue.

At the level of personal needs, members are trying to find a balance of openness (saying what they're really thinking and feeling) versus non-openness (withholding their real views). They're seeking a balance they feel comfortable with; one that lets them form closer relationships without too much risk of being exploited or getting hurt. What's the purpose behind the search for greater openness? It's the quest for *trust*. Trust in others' motives. Trust that what others say is what they mean. Trust that what others declare they'll do, they will do. Trust that if you make yourself vulnerable by admitting you haven't understood something or have made a mistake or don't know the answer, others won't attack you.

From the team's angle, greater openness prepares members for the discipline of *joint accountability*.

Joint accountability has two facets. The first is accepting responsibility for your part while holding your colleagues responsible for theirs. This means being ready to challenge underperforming colleagues to achieve better results. The second facet stops joint accountability degenerating into finger-pointing and blaming. You see, as well as holding themselves and teammates accountable for individual efforts, members also see themselves as jointly accountable for the whole team's results. As they see it, they succeed or fail as a team, meaning they won't allow post-event scapegoating.

However, at times, members will point out examples of underperformance, which means straight talking, which takes us back to openness. Will people feel comfortable enough (and care enough) to be that open in pursuit of collective results? That's the nub of the Combine issue.

Team purpose and goals

Defining the team's main goal is a key task in Commit. Making sure it remains relevant and motivating is important in Combust as it can partly offset self-esteem-driven problem behaviours by supplying an "emotional glue". However, when the Combine issue dominates the agenda, the team's purpose (reflected in its number one goal) can no longer *partly* offset members' self-esteem-driven behaviours. It must become *at least* as powerful in influencing behaviour as their self-esteem deficits.

If it isn't – and it's not guaranteed – Combining won't occur. Yes, if members open up and build trust, the group becomes more cohesive, which is essential to resolving Combine. But remember what I said earlier in this book: cohesion alone won't deliver Real Team results. Members of an aspiring Real Team must build openness and trust while seeing the team's aims as their own and hold one another jointly accountable if they're to navigate the Combine challenge successfully. For that to happen, the team's purpose must motivate all members. They must want to achieve their common goal while feeling it remains achievable. You can therefore see that although "team purpose and goals" is central to Commit, it cuts across all three C-C-C issues.

Team composition

You may not see a "who should be in the team?" question in Combine. But it can appear when – despite members' openness, cohesion and shared dedication to the goal – the team feels stuck on the upward curve and suspects it's missing key knowhow or needs fresh viewpoints and mindsets. That's when you'll find members thinking, "Do we need to add or replace members?"

Members' early questions

In chapter 7's overview, I distilled the questions that team members ask themselves in Combine to two issues. (1) *Am I ready to trust the people here and say what I really think, feel, want and intend, even at the risk of making myself vulnerable, or shall I remain guarded?* (2) *Shall I put the team's priorities before my own interests and, if so, given what we need to achieve, how can I best use my talents to help us succeed ... or shall I look after number one?* But as before, they mask important subtleties, so I'll list the more detailed questions they represent:

- How safe is it to reveal my real thoughts and feelings in this team?
- Are people telling the truth here?
- Do I trust these people? Who can I trust here?
- Can I – and do I want to – build closer, trusting relationships here?
- How much do I *need* to reveal here?
- How much of myself do I *want* to reveal here?
- Will they reject me if I'm too open about what I think isn't going well?
- Can I be myself and still be liked?
- So how open should I be with them?
- Do I care enough about our purpose and my colleagues to put team interests before my own?
- What's the best way of achieving our goals?
- What contribution to progress and results does the team need from me?
- What are my personal growth chances here?
- How can I balance my personal growth needs with what others want and, also, the whole team needs?

Members' focus

Here we see a distinct shift from the Commit and Combust challenges. In Commit, each member's focus is inward towards personal safety – it centres on "my" feelings and what I suspect team colleagues feel about "me". In Combust, it remains inwardly focused, this time on "my" goals, "my" feelings about "my" power here, and goals that help "me". In Combine, we again see an inward focus initially, but after time it's joined by an outward focus. Eventually, you should see a blending of the two focal points.

The inward phase usually comes early in Combine. Personal safety is still important. Secretly, members question if colleagues are telling the truth, being genuine, or whether they sense "hidden agendas" (unspoken selfish motives). They wonder about their team colleagues. Do they like them? Do they want to feel closer to them? But closeness (or intimacy as I called it in chapter 7) demands openness, so they consider how ready they are to reveal their real thoughts and feelings. If Combine goes well, they build trust – trust in fellow members' motives.

The outward focus centres on team goals, team success, joint results and joint emotions. Members focus on helping the team achieve its goal because they feel team success is more important than individual wins. It's not that they sacrifice their personal desires. Rather, they recognise a chance for personal growth and fulfilment through the team's journey and triumph. They've reached a "One for all and all for one" attitude. This is when you'll hear teammates saying, "We succeed as a team or fail as a team". Yes, as I've already said, they'll hold themselves jointly accountable, causing helpful peer pressure to become part of their culture, but this "we're all in it together" ethos means it won't turn into finger-pointing or blaming.

By blending their inward and outward attention the members keep their eye on the team's goal above all. While individual needs and continued trust remain important, joint results and shared success become the focus. Now the Potential Team is well on its way to becoming a Real Team. If the degree of collaboration climbs to where members display an unusually high personal commitment to the mission and one another's support, success and growth, a High-Performance Team can emerge.

Relationships and roles

For each member, Commit was about sensing a satisfying role. The emphasis in Combust was on settling into that role. Both reflected "my needs". By Combine, you should (if it's going well) see members adjusting their earlier roles if they don't suit and begin being more flexible in the roles they play – to better effect from the team's angle. They're not adjusting and flexing their roles just to suit themselves; they're also doing it to meet the team's needs. By now they're starting to see the team's needs as *our* needs.

In parallel, relationships have shifted.

In Commit, members' felt dependent on their colleagues' body language and remarks towards them for feelings of emotional security. They felt pressure to "fit in" with the team before considering what they wanted for themselves. In Combust, they pushed for greater independence as they struggled to define a role and achieve the influence they wanted. They were more likely to ignore others' wishes, deny their need for emotional support and concentrate on what *they* wanted. It's oversimplifying, but you could see the shift in Combust as an over-correction to the emotional dependence they experienced in Commit.

| **Commit** | | **Combust** | | **Combine** |
| Dependence | ➡ | Independence | ➡ | Interdependence |

In Combine, they realise they're "in it together", that they need each other's skills, experience and goodwill. Members no longer feel driven to "fit in" or ignore their colleagues' interests in favour of their own. Instead, they think and act in ways that recognise their own wishes while caring about teammates' needs. In other words, the dependence (of Commit) and independence (of Combust) morphs into interdependence in Combine. If Combine unfolds successfully, team members increasingly accept their practical two-way dependence on one another if they're to achieve their joint goals. Yet they continue expressing their individuality, but in ways that boost the team's results.

Members' typical behaviour

You'll see a major shift in members' behaviours in Combine compared with what you saw as they addressed the previous two challenges. In Commit, you could summarise the behaviour as "orientation and testing". In Combust, as "struggle and conflict". But if Combine unfolds successfully, you'll see more genuinely open exchanges. Members will express warm feelings, caring behaviour and strong support for one another, without ducking issues. You'll hear controversial opinions and deeper emotions, whether that's comfortable or uncomfortable for the team members. All this leads to members putting the team's goals ahead of their own selfish interests, plain speaking, closer bonds, selfless collaboration, strong peer pressure to deliver, tough two-way questioning, and better results. Genuine teamwork, in other words. Specific examples of helpful behaviour you'll see in Combine include:

- Helping colleagues with information, contacts and emotional support.
- Challenging one another's ideas and efforts, holding colleagues accountable regardless of status or experience, without scapegoating.
- Giving positive feedback to build colleagues' confidence.
- Listening to what colleagues are *actually* saying, not what you *think* they're saying.
- Making smart choices (not trying to do everything at once).
- Breaking down silos to share budgets, time and people.
- Joint problem solving, planning and decision-making.
- Joint implementation of decisions (not always working in silos).
- Embracing conflict and meshing differing views into decisions they all support.
- Naming the "elephant in the room".
- Working on their growth as a team, perhaps by learning new skills together.
- Combining skilfully to connect with and influence their key external audiences.

The second behaviour in this list most obviously represents joint account-ability in action. Joint accountability is a team's acid test. It's also the key test of the Combine challenge. You can't have a Real Team without it. Joint accountability emerges when openness, intimacy and high commitment to team purpose fuse to create team spirit. It shows as a blend of strong peer pressure to perform well, encouragement, direct (sometimes challenging) feedback, shared leadership, delight at joint successes, and collective pain when things don't go well. In short, if joint accountability isn't beginning to develop, you can be sure Combining isn't happening.

That said, I don't want to over-stress the "direct feedback" part of joint accountability because in my experience its silent counterpart – peer pressure to deliver – is the more powerful accountability driver. This means such feedback is seldom needed, but you'll see it when it is.

Joint accountability is different to what you'll see in Performance Groups where the leader holds everyone accountable. In Real Teams, *all* members hold themselves and everyone else accountable. This means members won't wait for the official leader to call out someone for continued poor attitude or behaviour. They'll do it themselves. You see this often in elite sports teams: everyone takes responsibility for applying this team discipline.

It's not easy to achieve joint accountability in business because individualism often reigns – above all at the top of companies – and it's not comfortable for many executives, especially those who aren't used to the five following challenges. One, making commitments to their peers. Two, being open to review and challenge by peers on what they've done or failed to do. Three, having to face opposing arguments. Four, receiving pressure from peers for improved results. Five, having to challenge colleagues, including those with higher status or who've been in the business longer. So joint accountability can be unfamiliar or downright threatening to some. That's why Combine is such a challenge for would-be business teams, especially senior teams.

Members' behavioural preferences

Team members' natural attitude to expressing their real thoughts and feelings will affect what happens in Combine. You'll see some people quick to open up because they enjoy relationships where they can air their feelings, innermost thoughts and perhaps their secrets. They want at least one person to confide in. Others choose to keep things impersonal, preferring more arm's-length relationships, although – and this is key – they'll open up when needed. The point is, people have different attitudes towards saying what's on their mind. As with the previous two issues, this confuses the picture, making it harder for members to judge whether it's safe to be honest or challenge their colleagues.

Members' self-esteem complications

Because Combine doesn't always go well, you often won't see the helpful behaviours listed in the "typical behaviours" section, mainly (but not entirely) because of self-esteem problems. You may recall the first basic Combine question: *Am I ready to trust the people here and say what I really think, feel, want and intend, even at the risk of making myself vulnerable, or shall I remain guarded?*

How members answer this question depends partly on their natural behavioural preferences in Combine, but also on their self-esteem. The self-esteem issue in Combine is no longer "significance" or "competence", but *likeability*: how likeable each member thinks they are. If, deep down, we see ourselves as unlikeable, someone people will reject if they get to know us, we'll find the Combine issue difficult. Why might we see ourselves as unlikeable? Usually because we believe we have character flaws making us unattractive, meaning no one would want to get close to us – perhaps we see ourselves as selfish, mean, dull, boring, jealous, ruthless, greedy, resentful or angry. Or sometimes because we've committed acts we feel guilty about, things we cannot forgive ourselves for.

Why does being unlikeable make Combine difficult for such a person? It's because Combine relies on open, honest, candid conversation. A member seeing him or herself as unlikeable will be anxious to avoid opening up because they'll be "revealed" as the person they think they are. Why anxious? Because they're convinced they'll feel the pain of rejection. Rejection is their great fear. They'll feel driven – as in Commit and Combust – to behave in ways that defend against their fear, which means they'll lose their ability to choose their natural openness behaviour at will. As before, we can classify people's behavioural defences in Combine along a bipolar scale:

Defences Against Being Rejected

Underpersonal behaviour   Overpersonal behaviour

Underpersonal behaviour is what you'll usually see, especially in leadership teams. Here, members avoid being open with anyone, even when it would help them and the team to share their thoughts and emotions. They keep their relationships distant and superficial; even cold if necessary. They want to avoid emotional connection and feel most comfortable when others behave similarly. "Let's keep things professional," they'll say. This way, they avoid rejection by ensuring the risk of revealing who they are (in their eyes) can't arise. After all, if you're not revealing your real thoughts and feelings, people won't realise how unlikeable you are, or so this "psychological script" runs. A more subtle version of underpersonal behaviour is being superficially friendly with everyone but open (and close) to no one. It can be a long time before people realise they don't really understand the member playing this game.

I see overpersonal behaviour less often in executive teams. This is, typically, where members make their thoughts and feelings – especially their feelings – known repeatedly, hoping colleagues will respond in kind. They over-share. They need others to like them. Their subconscious idea is that if they reach out – by being ultra-open and drawing like-minded people to them – they'll avoid their great fear of rejection. To gain approval they'll be intimate and confide in team colleagues, often on confidential or sensitive subjects, even when this may hurt the team or how others see them. As with underpersonal behaviour, they feel driven to behave like this to protect themselves against the fear of people rejecting them. A more subtle, more manipulative, more possessive version of overpersonal behaviour is to hold colleagues close, hog their attention and punish their efforts to build close relationships with others in the team.

Again, despite being polar opposites, *both underpersonal and overpersonal behaviour are just alternatives to dealing with the same fear: rejection.* The trouble is, the more common defence – underpersonal behaviour – means people don't say what's on their minds. This in turn means trust and joint accountability is slow to develop, which delays resolution of Combine.

Members who feel genuinely likeable won't behave so defensively. They're not driven by fear of rejection. They'll be equally comfortable getting close to others or remaining at a distance. They can handle another member's dislike without taking it to mean they're innately unlikeable; that everyone dislikes them. Some prefer to get closer to teammates, others prefer more distance, but they flex their behaviour to suit their own and the team's needs.

Problems to watch out for

It's common to see members being reluctant to say what they're really thinking and feeling until they get their bearings on their teammates. The problem is when this persists. But it's not the only unhelpful symptom to look for in Combine. Watch out for:

- Expressions of envy or jealousy including perhaps: undue focus on a teammate's flaws, mistakes or failures; adopting an icy tone; excluding someone from emails; or frequent quarrelling.
- An atmosphere of distrust.
- "Hidden agendas" (where members have selfish undeclared motives opposing the team's aims or best interests).
- An "elephant in the room" (an important problem everyone knows about but no one's prepared to name).
- A reluctance to open up and hold fellow members accountable, even in the face of poor behaviour, unacceptable attitudes or below-par results.
- Avoidance of conflict – even when conflict is exactly what's needed.
- Sabotage: the group "agrees" to do something, but then you see slow, sloppy or no follow-through, and perhaps secretive complaining in corridors.
- Complacency: where they tell themselves, "We're the best" while results are starting to slide.
- Groupthink: where the team puts so much stress on harmony and

unity they agree to goals and plans they know, deep down, are foolish. But no one dares challenge these decisions for fear of looking like the "odd man out" or the "awkward" or "disloyal" member. (I described groupthink in more detail in chapter 3. There is further detail in the appendix, *The Hidden Psychology of Teams*.)

- Closed or rigid mindsets: where the team thinks it knows all the answers and won't accept new viewpoints or data even when there's trouble ahead. This can accompany groupthink.
- Arrogance or hostility towards other groups, perhaps in the same company, causing unhelpful conflict and failure to collaborate.
- Stressing internal harmony while failing to connect with and influence key audiences outside the team like employees, customers or shareholders.

Resolution of issue

If Combine unfolds successfully, members get comfortable with speaking their minds in pursuit of the team's goals. They respect colleagues' feelings while refusing to avoid issues. Thus, they balance cohesion with a strong focus on joint results.

Team members can strengthen this balance by creating a virtuous circle. A "virtuous circle" is a chain of helpful events where one leads to another and another, reinforcing the first event, resulting in a continuous upward spiral. As you'll see in figure 17, members balance their openness and intimacy with dedication to team purpose, making them hold one another jointly accountable. That's when the virtuous circle can start. Joint accountability drives follow-through on decisions. Continued follow-through builds members' mutual trust and respect and a peer pressure to keep delivering... which reinforces joint accountability. This serves to drive the team through Combine, up the curve to Real Team and, possibly, beyond to High-Performance Team.

Am I implying that resolution of Combine has lower and higher stages? Yes. The lower stage results in a Real Team. The rare higher stage sees members become a High-Performance Team.

Figure 17: Combine's Virtuous Circle

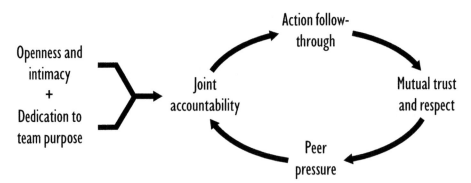

In the lower stage you'll see openness, trust and joint accountability, creating a strong team spirit where members put the team's interests first unless there's a personal emergency. You'll also see shared leadership even though there's a formal leader. In the rare higher stage, the gains of the lower stage remain, but the team has moved on. Now you'll see members:

1. Showing extraordinary commitment to the goal. To them it's more like a cause; they're pursuing a mission that's far greater than their selfish interests. This brings them an exceptional sense of purpose, focus and fulfilment.
2. Displaying remarkable personal commitment to helping one another succeed, and, just as important, grow in their team roles as they face tough moments together.
3. Sharing leadership to the point where it's hard to tell who the leader is when they're in action.

In summary, so you have the same easy-to-grasp summary that I gave you for Commit and Combust, look for these five signs of resolution in Combine:

- The members trust one another's motives, which shows as their readiness to say what they're really thinking and feeling on important, even sensitive issues.

- The members have grown emotional bonds, pulling them closer together as a team.
- You see examples of members putting the team's aims before their personal needs, for example, "turf" or career interests.
- The members have grasped "shared leadership" and are applying it, especially through the principle of joint accountability.
- The team consistently arrives at clear decisions and follows through skilfully.

Seeing the Big Picture

Having studied the Commit, Combust and Combine issues at close quarters, let's stand back and summarise the ground we've covered using the overview table you'll see in figure 18. That way you'll see the big picture without losing sight of the key details.

Figure 18: Overview of Commit-Combust-Combine Model

	Commit	**Combust**	**Combine**
Themes	Inclusion	Power	Intimacy and Focus
Individual drives and concerns	To be part of something bigger than you, to be noticed, to feel significant and included, to feel a distinct valued individual.	To feel competent, influential, able to cope and make a difference, to win others' respect for your efforts.	To be liked and build closer trusting relationships while both contributing to team goals and achieving personal growth.

continued overleaf...

Figure 18 continued...

	Commit	Combust	Combine
Key questions	Given our purpose, what blend of knowhow and behavioural skills do we need, and so who should be in this team? Shall I be an active, engaged member of this team or shall I stay uninvolved, hold back and remain on the sidelines?	Am I seeking high or low influence, especially when we consider and act on team decisions, and will I face battles with my colleagues, so shall I act timidly, subtly or forcefully?	Shall I trust these people and say what I really think and feel, at the risk of making myself vulnerable, or remain guarded? Shall I put the team's priorities before my own interests and, if so, how can I best use my talents to help us succeed ... or shall I look after number one?
Team purpose and goals	Must motivate all members enough to decide they're "in".	Must create enough "glue" as power struggles start.	Must be as powerful as self-esteem in shaping behaviours.
Each member's focus	Inward. My personal safety. My visibility. My feelings... and theirs about me.	Inward. My goals. My role. My impact. My power. Goals that help me. My feelings.	Inward and then outward. Me- trust-us. Joint outputs. Team goals and success. Our feelings.
Roles	Sensing my role(s)	Establishing my role(s)	Adjusting and flexing my role(s)
Relationships	Dependence	Independence	Interdependence
Behaviours	Orientation and testing	Struggle and conflict	Openness and collaboration

	Commit	Combust	Combine
Self-esteem complications	Fear of being *ignored or dismissed* due to believing that you are insignificant or inferior to those you are working alongside.	Fear of being *humiliated* because of failure, mistakes or not knowing the answers due to believing you are not good enough, an impostor.	Fear of being *rejected* if you say something fellow members object to, due to believing you're unlikeable, that people will never trust or like you.
Problems to watch out for	Superficiality, not paying attention, withdrawal, withholding, lateness or absence, pairing up.	Passive-aggressive silences, competition, cliques, conflict, avoiding issues, dominant members, scapegoating.	Distrust, complacency, hidden agendas, elephant in the room, closed or rigid mindsets, groupthink, sabotage.
Resolution of issue	Members feel included, they sense their role, they believe the team's aim is worthwhile and achievable, and they're "in".	Members settle into their team role, accept how decisions are made, and are happy with their influence and responsibilities.	Members open up, tell the truth, develop closer bonds, put the team's purpose first, and apply joint accountability.

Tools

Finally, if you'd like to start using your understanding of Commit, Combust and Combine, I'll give you a set of tools drawn from this chapter's content to help you start figuring out which C-C-C issue is to the fore in your team.

The first helps you work out if Commit is in force (meaning it's the dominant psychological issue in your team) or if you've resolved it and moved on. Box one lists indicators that it's still dominant. Box 2 itemises signs that you've resolved it enough for now.

The second and third do the same for Combust and Combine.

Suggests COMMIT Is Still in Force	Suggests Resolution of COMMIT

• Superficial conversations.
• It's all talk and little or no action.
• Members not paying attention.
• Members withdrawing or wanting to withdraw.
• Repeated lateness or absence.
• Members' body language suggesting they feel excluded.
• Members not speaking up even if they have a different opinion or perspective.
• Pairing up (mini cliques) and colluding for self-protection.
	Behaviour suggesting the team's members:
	• Believe the team's aim is sufficiently worthwhile and realistic.
	• Have assessed their teammates' reactions to them and feel included.
	• Can at least sense a value-adding role for themselves.
	• Have decided they want to stay and play their part in the would-be team …
	  at least for now.
	  (Note: bullet four stems from the first three points)

Suggests COMBUST Is Still in Force	Suggests Resolution of COMBUST
• Members competing to act as overall leader. • Over-long talks on how to approach tasks. • Dominant members intimidating colleagues. • Submissive members pretending to agree. • Awkward passive-aggressive silences. • Blaming and scapegoating. • Cliques competing against one another. • More powerful members presenting decisions to colleagues that were taken off-line in private. • Anger and accusations. • Overt rebellion. • Dip in commitment to original team goal. • Non-existent follow-through or chaotic or sloppy execution of so-called decisions.	Behaviour suggesting the team's members: • Have settled into team roles they find satisfying. • Have understood and accepted how the team reaches decisions. • Know who plays what role in those decisions. • Are satisfied with their own power and influence in the team (or at least most of them feel satisfied). • Feel good about their joint decisions judging by the skill and urgency they are showing in acting on them). • Believe a sense of order and structure has emerged from points one, two, three, four and five.

Suggests COMBINE Is Still in Force	Suggests Resolution of COMBINE
• Expressions of envy or jealousy. • An atmosphere of distrust. • "Hidden agendas" (selfish undeclared motives opposing the team's aims or best interests). • An "elephant in the room" (a big problem everyone knows about but no one names). • Reluctance to hold fellow members accountable, even in the face of poor behaviour, unacceptable attitudes or below-par results. • Conflict is avoided even when it's needed. • Sabotage: the group "agrees" to do something, but you see slow, sloppy or no follow-through, and perhaps secretive complaining in corridors. • Complacency: they tell themselves, "We're the best" while results are starting to slide. • Groupthink. • Closed or rigid mindsets. • Arrogance or hostility towards other groups. • Stressing internal harmony while failing to connect with and influence outside audiences.	• Members are building strong bonds and helping teammates with data, contacts and emotional support. • High trust — they embrace conflict and mesh differing views into decisions they all support. • Challenging one another's ideas and efforts, holding colleagues accountable regardless of status or experience, without scapegoating. • Giving positive feedback to one another. • Listening to what teammates are actually saying, not what they think they're saying. • Sharing budgets, time and people (no silos). • Joint problem solving, planning, decision-making, shared leadership and strong follow-through. • Joint implementation of decisions (not always working in silos). • Naming the "elephant in the room". • Working on their growth as a team. • Members are combining skilfully as a team to connect with/influence their external audiences.

The Key Points...

- This chapter's aim was – along with chapters 7 and 9 – to create the base for the diagnostic TeamFixer® tool I'll describe in Book Three.

- The C-C-C model is designed to help you grasp what's happening psychologically below the surface amid the emotional hurly-burly and behavioural confusion of team life. The model introduced three psychological issues: Commit, Combust 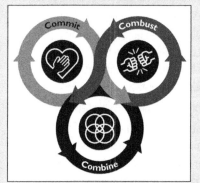 and Combine. They can follow the C-C-C sequence, but don't always, because "micro issues" can cause reversion to an earlier psychological challenge. That's why the infinity loop diagram shows the team's energies flowing from Commit to Combust and then on to Combine, but sometimes from Combust back to Commit and on occasions from Combine to Commit. Complicating things further, as the diagram shows, it's possible that mature teams, having slipped from Combine to Commit due to a micro issue can, once it's resolved, jump straight back to Combine.

- Having understood the basics in chapter 7, we examined the Commit-Combust-Combine model in more detail to reveal its subtleties and nuances.

- Commit:

  - Commit starts with appointing the new members. Ideally, this question will drive the selections: "Given our basic purpose, what blend of skills, knowhow and behavioural styles do we need, so who should we pick for this team?"

- However, most business work groups assume "blend of skills and behavioural styles" means "job titles" so they can end up lopsided and dysfunctional. This is why I recommended you look into Meredith Belbin's work. His research uncovered nine team roles reflecting distinct value-adding clusters of behaviour. We'll return to this in chapter 16.

- The team's basic purpose, its reason for being, will influence people selection, but you need a more measurable, *motivating*, shorter-term goal if the new members are to engage fully with their challenge. Defining this goal is a "must" if your team is to navigate Commit successfully. It provides the early emotional glue. You'll learn how to craft such a goal in Book Two.

- The word "motivating" is crucial. Members must see the goal as worthwhile (ideally inspiring) and achievable. They must *care* about it if they are to commit.

- After selection, people start wrestling with the subconscious question, "Should I be an active, engaged member of this team or shall I stay detached, hold back and remain on the sidelines?"

- Although members will get work done during Commit, their real focus will be inward, on their emotional comfort and safety.

- You will often hear superficial conversations while Commit is dominant. They serve a purpose: they allow members to learn about one another.

- Team members' natural preferences around engaging with new people will differ, making it hard for them to read one another, making it tougher to resolve Commit. Complications arising from self-esteem issues distort the natural preferences, causing misreading of others' behaviour, which then makes the issue even harder to resolve.

- The big self-esteem issue in Commit is self-significance. Team members often feel inferior or unworthy to be in the team. Their great fear is being ignored or feeling excluded. Why? Because it will confirm their insignificance. This fear drives them to adopt defensive patterns, making it harder to resolve Commit.

- Certain repeated problem behaviours are typical of Commit. I listed eight examples.

- Resolution of Commit comes after you've chosen a good enough people blend, when members can sense value-adding role for themselves, when they feel included based on other's reactions to them, when they believe the team's aim is worthwhile and achievable, and therefore they've thrown their hat in the ring (at least for now).

- I know I'm repeating myself, but if you've grasped that a team's purpose and goals are powerful drivers in deciding whether it resolves Commit successfully, you are correct. Agreeing a genuinely motivating common purpose and number one goal will make a huge difference to your success in addressing Commit quickly.

- Combust:

  - Once members have sufficiently resolved the second Commit question with a "Yes, I'm in" (at least for now), they ask themselves subconsciously, "Am I seeking high or low influence, especially when we consider and act on team decisions, and will I face battles with my colleagues, so shall I act timidly, subtly or forcefully?"

- The team's purpose and goals aren't central to resolving Combust, but they do help provide an emotional glue if they motivate all members.

- As in Commit, although members will pay attention to their task, their focus will still be inward as they try to fulfil their power needs. Their need for power will vary, making it harder for members to read one another. Some like to give orders; some like to receive orders. Some like to be obviously powerful; others prefer a more subtle "power behind the throne" role. Some want autonomy; others are readier to join forces.

- During Combust it is usual to see a power struggle, whether overt or covert. Self-esteem problems, which are common, only complicate the power struggles.

- The self-esteem issue centres on members' sense of competence. Many team members feel they're not good enough, that they won't be able to cope, that they'll be exposed as an impostor. They think they fear failing or making a mistake or not knowing the answer, but in fact their real fear is the emotional sting accompanying that experience – the pain of humiliation. Thus, they feel driven to adopt defensive patterns to avoid it, which only complicates the team's ability to resolve Combust.

- The power struggles and self-esteem complications can show up as the problem behaviours I listed on pages 135–136.

- Members have addressed this issue enough when they've settled into satisfying team roles, they've understood and accepted how they reach decisions, they feel comfortable with their degree of influence, and a sense of order and structure has emerged.

- Combine:

  - After members resolve the Combust issue sufficiently to create a sense of order, they pose two questions: "Am I ready to trust the people here and say what I really think, feel, want and intend, even at the risk of making myself vulnerable, or shall I remain guarded?" and "Shall I put the team's priorities before my own interests and, if so, given what we need to achieve, how can I best use my talents to help us succeed … or shall I look after number one?"

  - It's in Combine that a strong sense of "we" emerges. The emotional dependence of Commit and independence of Combust turns into interdependence.

  - Psychologically, it's the most complex of the three issues. Members have to balance their personal needs against the team's needs by learning to say what they're really thinking and feeling to build a climate of trust and joint accountability. That's not easy.

  - At first, members' focus will still be inward, centred on safety ("is it safe to make myself vulnerable here by admitting mistakes or things I don't understand?"), but gradually it must morph into an outward focus, towards the team's priorities, feelings and success.

  - If Combine is going well, you will see several helpful behaviours, all of which you can put under one heading: collaboration. This doesn't mean people are being "nice" to one another because it can mean direct challenges – especially in applying the principle of joint accountability, the acid test of this issue.

  - Joint accountability shows as a blend of mutual encouragement, strong peer pressure to perform well, direct (sometimes challenging) feedback and shared leadership. As I remarked in the main body of the text, I don't want to overstress the "direct feedback" aspect because that could promote the image of Real Teams as frightening hothouses of finger-pointing. They are not. The powerful peer pressure to perform well – a key feature of Combine – means you seldom need such feedback. But when you need it, you'll see it, because teams navigating Combine successfully accept that such directness is natural.

- Openness is the great behavioural challenge here. As in the previous two issues, people's natural preferences vary. Some people crave close relationships and will open up quickly. Others naturally prefer to deal with colleagues at arm's-length. The varying preferences make it harder for team members to figure out how safe it is to tell the truth as they see it.

- You'll see several unhelpful symptoms when this issue is dominant, which I listed on pages 146–147. Many are driven by members' self-esteem complications.

- The self-esteem issue in Combine centres on team members' fear of being judged unlikeable. In my experience, many managers see themselves as unattractive for one reason or another, meaning they fear rejection. This fear drives them to do whatever they can to stop others disliking or distrusting them. Their most common defence is to avoid opening up, which usually works against resolution of Combine.

- For success in Combine, the team's purpose and goals must become at least as powerful in influencing team members' behaviour as their self-esteem deficits.

- It's possible the team can become too much of a closed

system, in which case it will need fresh expertise and perspectives to avoid groupthink. Thus, the question of team composition can often reappear during Combine.

- There are five signs of resolution. One, members feel safe to say what they're really thinking and feeling without fearing embarrassment, attack or criticism. Two, they trust one another's motives and dependability. Three, as a result, their emotional bonds have grown and deepened. Four, they're putting the team's goals ahead of their selfish interests. Five, they're applying the discipline of joint accountability.

• Only after members address the Combine challenge sufficiently will you see a Real Team emerge.

• It's not easy for members to resolve the three C-C-C issues. They'll have different natural behavioural preferences in Commit, Combust and Combine, making it tougher for them to understand one another. Moreover, their self-esteem challenges will drive them to behave unhelpfully, complicating the picture further and impeding progress unless team members know what's happening and consciously address the problems. That's why the C-C-C model can be such a helpful aid to teams trying to climb the curve.

• Self-esteem complications may provide your greatest barrier in taking the would-be team up the curve. You can mitigate their effects by making sure the team's purpose and goals provide a powerful emotional glue throughout the Commit-Combust Combine journey.

9

Seeing Through the Fog III: Evolution and Endings

The Other Side of the Mountain

Few if any write-ups on team building discuss what happens after Potential Teams reach (*if* they reach) the Real Team position. They're like mountain climbing stories with "happily-ever-after" endings. But they don't tell the whole story. It's not real life. You could say the upward Team Progression Curve, underpinned by the C-C-C model, describes the mountain's north face. But like any mountain it has a south face. That means a downward curve is possible, even likely.

You'll see two kinds of downward curve depending on the team's lifespan.

Some teams have a limited lifespan. They know, at least roughly, when they'll disband. A project team fits this category. They have a deadline to achieve ("launch the XYZ product by the end of January") or a target to meet ("design a stylish electric family car with a battery range of 600 miles that we can price at £30,000"). The members know they'll disperse once they've achieved their mission.

Other teams don't. They continue indefinitely. Although the membership will change, they last as long as the organisation lasts. Examples include a company's top leadership team or a professional football club's first team.

Both indefinite-lifespan and limited-lifespan teams face the possibility or likelihood of a downward curve but for different reasons. The indefinite-lifespan team's downward curve, although common, is often slow, always unwanted, and depicts *performance decline as part of its longer-term evolution*. But for the limited-lifespan team, the downward curve is natural, expected and brief – it represents the team's *ending*. In this chapter we'll discuss both downward curves and their implications through the lens of the Commit-Combust-Combine model.

Long-Term Evolution

An indefinite-lifespan team's pathway doesn't work like a one-way ratchet. In other words, Real Teams can, with effort, up their game, raise their results, and occasionally (I stress, only occasionally) reach High-Performance Team status ... but they can also decline.

To be clear, we're not talking about micro issues here. Micro issues are brief relapses while the Potential Team is climbing the Progression Curve. Instead, we're talking about a new downward curve where something deeper, something more basic, has gone awry. Downward curves are longer term problems. Here, the team is no longer climbing, it's sliding downwards.

Figure 19: Possible Team Life Cycles

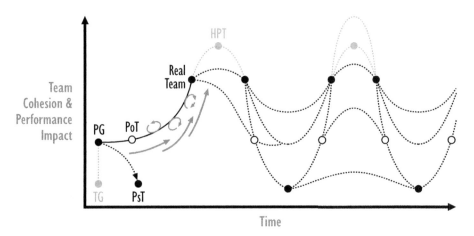

The diagram in figure 19 sketches an extended view of a team's possible evolution after reaching Real Team level. It has two important messages.

First, if a Potential Team climbs the curve and performs as a Real Team, it must work to stay there. There's no guarantee it will remain at that level. The diagram shows the paths it could take. Without addressing its problems, it could fall to Potential Team level or plunge to the Pseudo-Team position. Or dip slightly and recover. Or go on to scale new heights and redefine what's possible as a High-Performance Team... or anything between.

Second, it suggests most teams won't sustain their results evenly at Real Team level over several years. Note that I said "evenly". Teams can continue to perform well if they stay tuned to the C-C-C issues and seven action principles in Book Two, but dips and rises are likely. And, to repeat, steady decline is just as possible if they don't stay alert. Even the best teams experience ups and downs, as we see in professional sport. For example, Liverpool FC dominated English football from 1975 to 1990, winning the league championship 10 times in 15 years, but then waited another 30 years before winning their next title.

What causes a Real Team that's climbed the curve and become a robust solid unit to slip down the other side of the mountain? Here are twelve scenarios:

Scenarios Causing a Downward Curve

1 Arrogance
Prolonged success leads to complacency, arrogance and a habit of clinging to the status quo, blocking new insights and perspectives from outsiders, causing unhealthy "groupthink", recycling of the same old opinions, biases and, eventually, team blindness. Results slowly decline, often unnoticed until it's too late. *[Combine]*

2 Defence against dire threat
The team becomes too inward-looking not because of prolonged success but because it's facing what it sees as dire threats. It stops engaging with employees and customers with its previous consistency, skill and energy. The company's atmosphere dips, delivery of strategy becomes sloppy and results dive. *[Combine]*

3 Change of team leader
The team leader changes, bringing new values and beliefs, implicitly or explicitly, e.g. he or she may be uncomfortable with a Real Team's democratic style of working, instead preferring a Performance Group's hub-and-spokes approach, no matter the challenges facing the work group. *[Commit]*

4 New attitude from sponsors
People above the team change their views or feelings towards it (perhaps they view its mission differently now or they lose interest) and withdraw their support, causing team members' motivation to collapse. *[Commit]*

5 New selfish members
New members arrive who behave in ways that hinder the team's previous "one for all and all for one" mentality. *[Hard to classify as it depends on who's arrived and what's happening. It could be a Commit, Combust, or Combine problem.]*

6 Previous goal wears out
The team's purpose and aims change, perhaps because it's achieved its original goal or events have made the old goal irrelevant or it's forcing itself to act as a team when working as a Performance Group would be a wiser choice. *[Commit]*

7 Members leave
Key members leave or retire, leaving skills, mindsets and behavioural gaps, which the team doesn't fill. *[Commit]*

8 Underperformers indulged
One or more members continually underperform or misbehave but aren't removed from the team. *[Combine]*

9 Intense scandal
The team experiences an intense scandal or dispute among its members, leading to internal rifts. *[Combust or Combine]*

10 Major setback
The team experiences a major failure, creating fear and exposing unresolved self-esteem C-C-C issues, causing team members to forget their original purpose, leading to fear-driven behaviour. *[Commit, Combust or Combine]*

11 Series of smaller setbacks
The same as #10, but only after a continuous series of smaller failures or setbacks. *[Root issue could be Commit, Combust or Combine]*

12 New competitors or technologies
New rivals emerge, changing the game, exposing attitude, skill, or creativity gaps, meaning that unless the team replaces members, adds new ones, adopts new habits or learns new skills, it will face more problems. *[Commit]*

Clients have asked: how do you know if you're experiencing a micro issue (meaning it's only a brief slide on your way up the curve) or a descent down a new curve, what you could call a "macro issue", which is more serious? I answer that it's a question of duration, trend and difficulty to fix. Are you seeing steady or momentary decline? Is the problem relatively quick and easy to fix or is it more stubborn and complex? But in fact it doesn't matter whether it's a micro or macro issue, you approach it the same way: get a sense of where the problem lies (Commit, Combust or Combine) to narrow down your diagnosis, then identify your specific problems using the TeamFixer® tool in Book Three. Having done that, apply the key principles or techniques you'll read about in Book Two.

The big point is this: team members must stay alive to the C-C-C issues *and keep renewing their momentum if they are to become and stay a Real Team.* That's why the seventh of the action principles (Renew or End) in Book Two's 7P model is mostly about the "how" of team renewal.

Also, they mustn't become too disheartened if their results slip temporarily because that's common. The ideal is to minimise such dips – which the best teams do – and, if possible, surpass your previous level. But let's be clear; that's hard without a model to help you understand what's going wrong while it's happening and find a way to get back on track. That's what this book offers you.

Endings

In 1977, Bruce Tuckman revisited his 1965 Form-Storm-Norm-Perform model. He wanted to know if published research in the intervening 12 years had supported or undermined his four-stage model. After reviewing 22 group studies, he found that although only one had set out to test his model, they broadly supported his 1965 paper. But he noticed something else: many of the published analyses suggested a termination phase. He and his co-author decided this was an omission from their original model so they added a fifth stage they called "Adjourn". Thus, they recognised endings as a distinct stage in the lives of limited-lifespan teams. You will see a downslope when they end, but it will be unlike an indefinite-lifespan team's descent in four ways: it's planned, expected, steeper, and of shorter duration.

It fell to William Schutz, creator of the FIRO theory, to explain what happens below the surface when groups end. He believed their psychological challenges unfold in reverse order. This suggests that as Real Teams approach their end point, they will experience Combine, Combust and Commit in that order. You could see it like this:

Combine	With the Real Team's task nearing completion, its purpose becomes less all-consuming and all-important. Thus, the need for joint accountability weakens. The members can start thinking about their own goals again because it's no longer so important to put the team's aims before their personal priorities and ambitions. Then...
Combust	The members start turning their attention to future roles outside the team, meaning their existing team roles matter less and, with the end nearing, the need for conflict lessens. And...
Commit	Finally, with the goal achieved, their commitment diluted, and their roles no longer needed, the team disbands.

Putting aside the psychological mechanics, the main point here is that a limited-lifespan team's ending is another notable moment in its life cycle. I say that because endings matter for two reasons. First, a team's members who have worked intensively and achieved something important over, say 6–9 months or longer, can display problem behaviour as the ending approaches. Second, the companies employing them will see advantages to managing endings well.

What problems might you see in, for example, a successful project team and why do they arise? They occur because the members have created and become attached to a team identity, they've built close relationships and formed a strong sense of collective achievement. This means the impending

ending can bring a sense of imminent loss: it's the death of the team. For some members, the approaching ending won't prove difficult. But for others who dislike endings it can provoke sadness or anxiety, especially if they're about to leave an encouraging, fun, creative, achievement-orientated atmosphere and return to a more restrictive, staid working culture. They may seek unhelpful means of parting ways with colleagues that minimise their emotional discomfort. For example, you may see them try to avoid separation by keeping the team going, perhaps by delaying or prolonging work through absenteeism or lateness to keep the team intact. Or you'll see members failing to use their initiative, relying too much on the leader, which again slows things down. Sometimes you'll see certain members wanting to punish colleagues for slights or incidents they haven't forgotten or forgiven despite the team's success.[29]

The companies employing the team members can experience five advantages of managing endings well. One, good endings help cross-company cooperation when members return to their day jobs. If they feel good about the work they've done and camaraderie they experienced, they're more likely to build on their friendships as they return to their old jobs, which means you'll probably see stronger inter-department links. In this way, a series of successful teams can build a culture of collaboration. Two, well-managed endings are helpful for sending the cross-company message that working in limited-lifespan teams is both fulfilling and good for your career. Three, successful endings leave helpful memories that become positive collaboration stories and enter company folklore ("do you remember when...?"). Four, it's good for team members' confidence – they feel they've accomplished something worthwhile, they've been appreciated and they've built close enduring relationships – which means they're likely to perform better in their day jobs. Five, if you find lingering "hot" issues between certain members, it's a mistake not to iron them out before the team disbands because those same interpersonal problems could block inter-department collaboration later on.

If you're wondering how to manage a good ending and reap the benefits I've just described, Book Two's explanation of the seventh action principle, Renew or End (chapter 19) will offer you practical tips.

The Key Points...

- The life of a team doesn't end once it reaches the Real Team (or even High-Performance Team) position. For indefinite-lifespan teams, a downward curve is possible, even likely. So are occasional dips. For limited-lifespan teams, a downward curve is certain as it represents their ending.

- This means that if a Potential Team climbs the progression curve and reaches the Real Team position, it must work to stay there. There's no guarantee it will stay at that level.

- I've listed twelve causes of long-term dips or decline. I'm not saying they are the only scenarios; I list them to heighten your awareness of what may happen.

- Even the best teams dip at times. Spotting and limiting the decline is the key skill.

- The discipline of renewal is a must if real teams want to stay at the top of their game.

- Bad endings in limited-lifespan teams – for example, project teams – can have negative wider results for their sponsoring companies. It makes sense to manage team endings consciously and skilfully.

- Good endings can promote a collaborative cross-department culture across the company, to the point where that culture becomes part of its "secret sauce".

10

The Next Step

You've reached the end of Book One, the "what you need to *know*" part of this trilogy. At the start I suggested there were big payoffs for you and your company from learning how to build winning teams again and again. I argued you could even make it a competitive advantage. But I also stressed that team building isn't straightforward, which is why it helps to admit what you don't know and spend time on grasping the basics. If you've read until this page, you've done exactly that. You have:

- Seen the previously hidden psychological obstacles that mean you have to put effort in to build a team.
- Understood the Team Progression Curve, the six types of work group and the dangers of becoming a Pseudo-Team.
- Grasped the important contrast between Performance Groups and Real Teams and realised that not every challenge you face demands a team, that a performance group approach may sometimes be enough.
- Learned that genuine High-Performance Teams are rare, which is why it's more realistic to aim at Real Team status.
- Understood why so few senior management groups have become genuine teams ... and how that can change.
- Penetrated the emotional fog of team life to see the three psychological issues – Commit, Combust and Combine – that all teams face in climbing the curve.

- Studied the C-C-C issues enough to start figuring out which one is affecting your team most right now.
- Recognised that even successful indefinite-lifespan teams face what I called "the other side of the mountain". This is the hard reality that no team can stay at the top of their game without continual conscious renewal.
- Realised that limited-lifespan teams need to manage their endings successfully.

You're now ready for Book Two – the "what you need to *do*" instalment in this three-part series. It'll offer a seven-principle (7P) action model for taking you up the curve by nailing the C-C-C issues you've read about here.

You glimpsed this model towards the end of chapter 7 when I described the conditions you'd need to meet to reach Real Team status. You may recall I listed the conditions under seven headings. You'll find those headings match Book Two's seven principles. So you don't have to look back I've summarised them for you in this diagram:

The Seven-Principle Action Model

Book Two starts with the big picture: a high-level view of the 7P model. Then you have chapters on each of the seven principles. They offer detailed explanations with practical examples, frameworks, checklists and tips for putting each principle into action. The book closes by retelling the Apollo 13 story through the lens of the 7P model. You'll read how NASA teams applied the seven principles in extraordinarily testing circumstances.

Don't forget, you can read my articles, watch my videos or download my team building tools for free by signing up at the Leadership Mastery Suite website. Its address is **www.leadershipmasterysuite.com**. The downloadable tools from this first book are:

- A one-page outline of the Commit-Combust-Combine model.
- A simple one-page summary of the signs suggesting your team has resolved Commit, Combust or Combine or whether one of them remains in force.
- A PDF copy of the appendix, *The Hidden Psychology of Teams*. Why not share it with your team colleagues for awareness-building and discussion?
- A bonus tool (not mentioned in the text) to help you and your teammates figure out where your work group lies on the Team Progression Curve.

You'll also find Book Two and Book Three's tools there plus all the tools from my first book, *The Three Levels of Leadership*.

With that, I'll hand over to Book Two...

Appendix

The Hidden Psychology of Teams

This appendix supports Book One's chapter 1 in How To Build Winning Teams Again and Again, my three-part series on team building. There I outlined a simplified version of my Dual Forces model in explaining what happens psychologically below the surface in teams. Here I'll give a fuller account of the Dual Forces model with extra examples, mini case studies and technical notes.

It Takes Effort to Create Teams

Here's my big point up front: *it takes conscious effort to build teams to succeed and keep on succeeding because they face powerful, hidden, unhelpful psychological forces few people know about. To be blunt, if you don't attend to these forces, don't expect your group to become a team and perform like winners.*

To be clear, when I say, "it takes conscious effort to build teams", I'm talking specifically about teams, not work groups in general. You'll see three types of groups in the workplace: task groups, performance groups and real teams. If you imagine a "results scale", task groups sit at the bottom, performance groups in the middle and real teams at the top. Teams are the most ambitious, creative form of work group you'll find. I've given greater detail on the contrasts between the work groups in chapter 4, but to clarify what I mean by "real team", here's my definition: [30]

> A small group of people with complementary skills and roles who commit to a specific challenging common purpose, blend their abilities and hold one another accountable for delivering collective work outputs and results.

Although they deliver superb results, real teams don't form effortlessly. Yes, theoretically it's possible a team might emerge and endure easily if its members gel and they all see the problem or opportunity similarly. Possible, but unlikely, in my experience. Why? Two reasons.

One, real teams demand disciplines many people dislike. For example, members must hold teammates accountable for their behaviour and results, not expect their leader to do it all. They must also accept their interdependence by giving up some autonomy.

Two, when adults try to achieve results together you can expect trouble at some point. Again, why? Because when people work in teams, and especially when they feel under pressure, they create and unleash a complex array of hidden socio-psychological forces. The result? Unhelpful behaviour. The effect is like balls bouncing around a snooker or pool table, cannoning into one another, creating chaos, misdirection and unintended results. These hidden forces mean you can't expect a bunch of adults to act as a team and achieve ambitious aims simply because someone asks them to work together or they seem socially compatible.

In my view the second issue, the socio-psychological challenge, is the key factor because it's also the main driver behind reason one: team members' reluctance to accept interdependence and apply the discipline of joint accountability. So the first step in building successful teams is to understand these hidden socio-psychological forces.

Working in Teams Creates Anxiety

While coaching teams I sometimes ask members to score their assertiveness on a 0–10 scale. Zero means they are poor at saying what they want, when they want, how they want, and getting the response they want, while ten means they are good at asserting themselves. I give them two scenarios. First, they rate their assertiveness when working *one-to-one*. Then we add their scores. Next, I ask them to repeat the 0–10 self-scoring, but this time rating their personal assertiveness when *working in a team*. Again, we add their scores.

Guess which total is always lower. It's "the working in a team" score. Repeatedly, I find it's harder for most people to express their thoughts and feelings genuinely and skilfully when working in teams or small work groups. They say the conditions feel riskier than one-to-one working, causing them to experience a subtle but real anxiety that cramps their style.

Figure 1: Dual Forces Model
Individual and Collective Forces in Teams & Groups

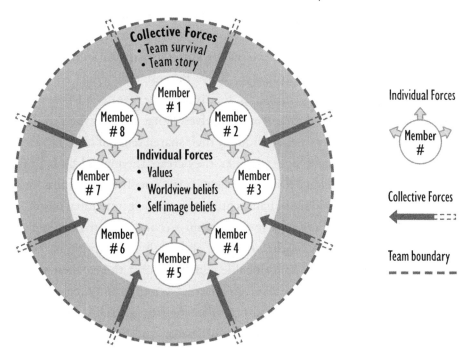

Dual Forces

Why? What's happening? Why does working in teams and small groups make us uneasy and limit our contribution?

Over one hundred years of research into groups and theorising by Wilfred

Bion, William Schutz, Irving Janis, Gustave Le Bon and others listed in the notes has led to numerous explanations.[31] And that's the problem. Try wading through their writings and you're likely to end up confused. Can we cut through the intellectual jungle to integrate and simplify their ideas? Yes, we can. By distilling their thinking we can see dual forces affecting us when working in teams and small groups. I call them the "Collective" and "Individual" forces. Together they form the Dual Forces model you see in figure 1.

- Collective forces stem from pressures created jointly by the team members.
- Individual forces flow from each member.

You might be thinking, "Isn't there another force coming from beyond the team, like company culture or pressure from competitors or perhaps the board of directors? Yes, it's true, those external pressures do exert an influence, but I don't include them as a third force. Why? Because their effect is filtered and controlled *by the Collective forces*, that is, *how the team as a whole views those outside sources*, not the sources themselves. What controls the way they view them? The members' beliefs, notably their shared sense of team identity, purpose, values and capability. Together, they create the mental filter I call the team's "story", which we'll study in the next section. The point for now is that this collectively held set of beliefs presses in on their individual minds.

For example, members of a football team striving to win the English Premier League may lack belief in their ability to be champions. Now imagine a referee awards a questionable penalty against them. Their shaky self-belief causes them to see the referee's verdict as unjust and themselves as victims. Their sense of victimhood magnifies their fragile self-belief, which drives a dip in their mental toughness and energy, and they end up losing. Now imagine another football team with deeper self-confidence aiming for the same trophy and, again, imagine a referee's doubtful penalty award goes against them. They also see his ruling as unjust, but their greater belief in themselves spurs them to increase their efforts... and they win.

The message? It's the same external event, but the team's collective attitude decides if and how it affects their play. So external events by themselves don't create the forces acting on teams. Instead, the team members create Collective forces through their perception of external events. Without realising, they create a shared psychological filter that presses in on them from outside their individual minds.

Note that I'm saying forces plural. The Collective and Individual forces have their own sub-forces. The Collective forces comprise the *story* and *survival* forces. The Individual forces encompass three sub-forces: the members' limiting *values*, their *worldview* limiting beliefs and their *self-image* limiting beliefs. You can see all five sub-forces in figure 1. We'll examine them closely in the next two sections and then see how they combine to create an effect I call the Emotional Combustion Chamber.

Collective Forces

The Collective forces emerge when, without realising, the team members create a *living system*.

Teams as living systems

We'll start by understanding how living systems form. Imagine a new eight-person team as illustrated in figure 2's example. The thin dotted arrows connecting the members reflect their early exchanges, their effects on one another and any emerging bonds. That's phase #1: the team or group's beginning.

When the team members repeatedly meet and work together, often without realising they create expectations, mindsets, norms of thinking and behaviour, emotional bonds, and habits. These combine to form a *living system*.

This is phase #2: emergence of the living system.

Note the term "living system" because both words are significant. A *system* arises when its elements interact to make a whole with a distinct identity and purpose that's greater than the sum of its parts. In other words, if you studied the parts separately you couldn't predict the system's characteristics and potential.

So, for example, a car is a system. Cars contain assemblies like engines, gearboxes and dashboard computers, and tiny components like screws and rivets, but what makes them cars is the way the parts work together to create a means of transport with a distinctive look and feel. The parts can't do that separately.

Figure 2: Formation of Teams as Living Systems

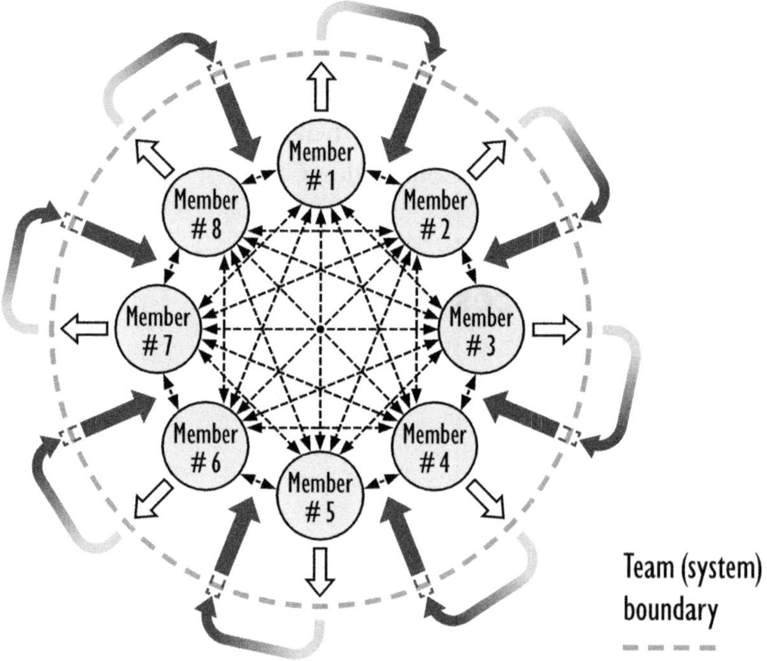

Team (system) boundary
- - - -

Phase #1

◀- - - - -▶

Beginning: people in a team (system) form relationships

Phase #2

⇨

The team's purpose, identity, capability and shared values plus individuals' relationships create a living system that wants to survive and enact its story

Phase #3

◀━━

The team's (system's) survival and story forces press in, affecting and shaping the members' thinking, feelings, behaviour and relationships

Teams and groups are also systems. Their members are the parts. When they interact they create, influence and preserve the system. But groups and teams aren't mechanical systems, they're *living* systems. Like all living systems they do whatever they can to adapt and survive.

As the team members talk, they gain a measure of their colleagues, which is when relationships start to form. They build a sense of who they are collectively (identity), what they stand for (values), what they want to achieve and why (purpose), and what they're capable of – which, together, I call their *story*, the first of the Collective forces. We can show it like this:

Team **story** = its shared sense of **identity**
+ **purpose**
+ **values**
+ **capability**

The "story force" spawns shared attitudes, beliefs, thinking habits and behavioural norms that, together, we call culture. These are the white arrows pointing out towards the team boundary (the dashed line circle) in figure 2.

From this the living system (team) develops its second force: the drive to *survive*. Now the living system wants to survive and live out its story. This is when the two Collective forces grow in strength. The combination of story and survival drives influences what the members think, feel and do, especially under pressure. The thick dark inward-pointing arrows in figure 2 depict this effect. This combined force adds a twist: although individuals unwittingly combine to create the living system, the system can, without them realising, come to control them in phase #3. It does so by distorting the culture, driving their behaviour in unexpected ways.

Having understood the living system at high level, we'll look closer at the "story" and "survival" forces to see how they influence the team members' behaviour.

Story force

The first Collective force, the team's "story", has powerful effects. As you see in figure 3, identity, purpose, values and capability combine to form a mental model – a story – that a team's members subconsciously absorb, accept and play out in action. (Bear in mind that although you'll see these four "story" elements in teams, they can apply equally to companies or even nations.) The story can develop quickly (within minutes) or slowly (over years). Similarly, its effects can recede quickly or persist for decades. I'll give you examples of each element:

- *Identity:* "we represent this city", "we stand for this cause", "we're the good guys fighting the evil they represent", "we are the senior leadership team".
- *Purpose:* "we're aiming to win the championship", "we'll crush the enemy", "we'll launch this new product on time", "we've got to save this business".
- *Values:* "no finger-pointing, we succeed or fail as a team", "the end justifies the means", "no egos, everyone matters here", "customer satisfaction before everything", "maximising shareholder value is our top priority".
- *Capability:* "we can win this race", "we can do this task", we're at our best when the pressure is on", "we're good but not good enough to win", "we have no chance".

Figure 3: The Two Collective Forces

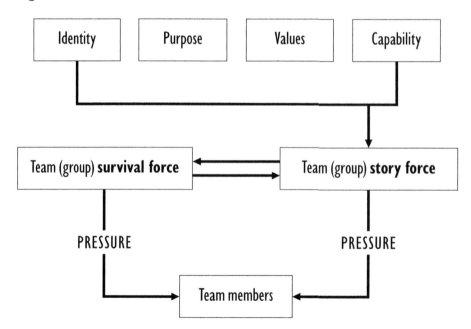

Note: teams or groups may decide their purpose or others – perhaps a company's owners, the board of directors or the government – may impose it on them. The purpose may arise slowly over years, decades or centuries or quickly over minutes, hours or weeks.

Problems arise when teams and groups develop unhelpful stories that grip them at certain moments – usually times of heightened emotion. This can cause two unhelpful effects. One, groups may behave aggressively in ways their members wouldn't consider if they were acting on their own. Two, they may perform well below their potential when facing pressures that play on their story fears.

Consider these two real-life examples of negative stories:

Aggressive immoral behaviour

Lynch mobs are groups bent on killing someone on the spot unlawfully. The mob may hold the target responsible for a serious crime, but sometimes the person has done nothing wrong. The target is focused on simply because he or she belongs to the "wrong" group – perhaps they have the wrong skin colour or practise the wrong religion.

The lynch mob's identity ("we are against them"), purpose ("we must kill them to remove the threat they represent"), values ("the end justifies the means") and capability ("we can do it now if we act together") creates enough anonymity and momentum for its members to overcome any moral doubts and act as one to carry out the execution.

An incident in 1857 demonstrated this lethal us-versus-them group thinking. Nine members of the Mormon Church's militia branch in Utah attacked a wagon train of emigrant families heading to California in a region called Mountain Meadows. The emigrants resisted for five days until the Mormons approached them with white flags signalling a truce. Being low on food and water they agreed to the truce and accepted the Mormons' offer to escort them out of the area so they could continue their journey. But after travelling a short distance the Mormon militiamen murdered the 120 men, women and children, burying them in shallow mass graves. Today, the Mormon Church preserves a monument in Mountain Meadows to honour those who died.

The killers, all members of a Christian religious group, acted in a way that almost certainly went against their individual moral standards. The incident showed what social psychologists have long known: groups can engage in behaviour that individuals wouldn't commit or tolerate. This happens when what I'm calling the "story" force presses in on members, pushing them to do something they wouldn't otherwise do.[32]

Collective underperformance

If a group or team's story is negative, its members may perform well below their ability when facing pressures that play on their story fears. It could be a one-off below-par display, like a sports team "freezing" in a final. But if the story spreads and remains unchallenged, it can endure for years.

I believe the England football team underperformed for decades because of its unspoken "story". Despite hosting the world's richest football league, England performed poorly in World and European Championships, winning only 6 knockout round games in finals in the 50 years up to 2016. Even more striking in those 50 years was England's dire record in penalty shootouts – the moment when individual players must hold their nerve. It won only 14% of these "sudden death" contests, putting it 30th in the world for success at shootouts, well below its average team ranking (10th) over that half-century. This dismal long-term picture reached its peak when Iceland, with a population of 330,000, the tiniest nation ever to reach the European finals, fought back from 1–0 down to outplay England and knock them out of the 2016 tournament.

England's play against Iceland was so poor in the second half that Steven Gerrard, an ex-England captain, and other experts reckoned a collective psychological weakness under pressure was causing England's continuing under-performance.[33] The then Belgium captain, Vincent Kompany, who played in the English Premier League, wrote in The Times the day after the game: *"I wasn't expecting that. I thought England would show their quality against Iceland, but what I saw was an extreme kind of collective failure. Looking from the outside, I honestly can't work out how it happened. What I do know is that when people respond by saying the players 'aren't good enough,' they are wrong. I've spent years playing against these players. They are much better than they appeared against Iceland. England had one of the strongest squads at Euro 2016 and yet something happened on Monday, a psychological 'event', to cause them to perform like that. It looked like something got to them."*

I believe Kompany and other experts were right.

Until 2016, I suspect England teams were living with an enduring story containing a powerful negative capability belief while lacking a long-term motivating purpose and supporting values.

The story may have been: "English fans expect us to do well because we're the nation that invented football (*identity*), so we'll do our best (*purpose*) but we're not good enough to handle tough moments in knockout games (*capability*) and when we fail they'll condemn us." While I don't know if this is their exact story, it fits Steven Gerrard's analysis, which you can read in endnote 33.

Alongside the corrosive capability belief ("not good enough"), note the watery purpose ("we'll do our best"). Note too the absence of values to give the players pride, energy and belief when joining the national squad. I suspect England will only perform consistently well in tournament finals when they recast and embody their story on and off the field.

My point is that a team's story – the first Collective force – can have huge adverse implications for its behaviour and results under pressure.

However, the reverse is also true – a powerful positive story can lift a team's performance. A great example is the New Zealand All Blacks who decided to recast their story in 2004. The result? They raised their historical win rate from 75% to 86% and won the Rugby World Cup in 2011 for only the second time in their history. They retained it in 2015. They stayed the world's top rugby team for another four years. Endnote 34 has more detail.[34]

Perhaps it won't surprise you to learn that crafting a positive story is one part of the 7P team building model I'll introduce in Book Two of *How To Build Winning Teams Again and Again*.

Survival force

I've explained that a group's members may yield to the system's pressure to live out its story by thinking and behaving in habitual ways. In this way they can lose their individual ability to choose freely and start reacting to events in ways they wouldn't do outside the team or group. The "survival" force can have a similar effect (often on an even wider scale) whenever the group feels threatened and its continued existence is in question.

Think about the behaviour of the Roman Catholic Church in the last five decades. Despite its Christian message, some priests molested and raped young parishioners in secret. When victims complained, what did the Church do? It went into survival mode. Bishops told themselves the church's image came first and justice second. Thus began a worldwide cover-up. Yet this ran counter to the Church's spiritual mission and morals. Why did it happen? Because the living system's survival drive – its second Collective force – was controlling individuals' behaviour.

The Roman Catholic Church is an extreme but not unique example of the survival force at work. Consider the 2016 FIFA (football's world governing body) scandal where executive after executive tumbled from power with whistle-blowers and investigators exposing their fraud, cover-ups and false denials, which they'd justified to themselves as "protecting FIFA". The living system's pressure to survive caused individuals and even groups within FIFA to become stuck in foolish or disgraceful behavioural patterns.

The point is that through the survival force living systems can mimic Doctor Frankenstein's monster, meaning the creation becomes the oppressor, as happened in Mary Shelley's famous novel. Thus, the members yield to the living system's drive to survive. They do things external observers can see, but those inside cannot. Even if a minority do, they often feel powerless to change things because the urge to survive as a collective entity dominates the group's thinking.

Collective forces' effect on teams and small work groups

My overall point is this: the two Collective forces – which teams and groups create without realising – are real, powerful and often cause unhelpful effects.

So far I've offered examples of the Collective forces as they affect teams, groups and entire organisations in the fields of religion (Roman Catholic church, Mormon militiamen), civil injustice (lynch mobs) and sport (FIFA, England football and New Zealand rugby teams). But how do Collective forces typically show at work in leadership and project teams?

You normally see them when team members feel apprehensive. The team feels under pressure or threatened. Perhaps their results are poor or they're tackling a high-risk project or face external criticism. That's when the story and survival forces kick in, pressing in on the members.

Research and experience shows they may respond in one of six ways. The first four are survival-driven. The fifth flows from either the story or survival drives or a mixture of both. The sixth occurs when teams outplay their negative story.[35]

1. **Over-dependence on the leader:** Members over-rely on a charismatic leader to solve their problems and survive (think Margaret Thatcher, the former UK prime minister, with her Cabinet ministers in the 1980s). This means leaders can find themselves put on a pedestal and under pressure to supply energy, brilliant answers and wise choices for followers who

behave passively, denying their own will and ideas. However, real teams need all members to contribute their skill, energy, knowhow and creativity to making decisions and completing tasks, so leader dependency usually works against team success in the long run. That was true for Thatcher's Cabinet with its eventual split between "wets" (her label for ministers who opposed her policies) and "dries" (her supporters).

2. **Leader scapegoating:** The flip side of leader over-dependency. Dominant leaders put on a pedestal will eventually disappoint their followers because the expectations placed on them are unrealistic. They'll feel the backlash as scapegoating, hostility and rebellion, which may be overt or hidden. Followers blame the leader partly to absolve themselves ("our problems aren't my fault"), but mainly for the team's survival. It may or may not involve a fight, but they'll eventually replace the leader who's so disappointed them, returning to dependency on a new (hopefully more able) leader. Meanwhile attention to tasks and results often slips amid the upheaval. We saw leader scapegoating and rebellion with Margaret Thatcher in the late 1980s. It was also in evidence at Chelsea football club in the first half of the 2015–16 season when the team collapsed from being runaway champions the previous year to relegation candidates. The result: the manager, Jose Mourinho, lost his job and Chelsea eventually finished tenth, the worst performance by defending champions in twenty-four years. I have also seen a highly successful (if disagreeable) CEO toppled by leader scapegoating.

3. **Avoidance of issues:** A result of members' subconscious urge to keep the team intact and therefore survive by avoiding conflict at almost any cost. To do so members will dodge the issues they're meant to tackle and avoid bold decisions, but the delay often makes the unresolved issues worse.

4. **Groupthink:** Like "avoidance", the aim is survival through group togetherness. Unlike avoidance, instead of fudging issues

and delaying decisions, the team will agree to bold goals or plans that some members quietly disagree with but choose not to challenge, sometimes with disastrous results for the team. Other members may discourage colleagues from expressing opposing views or even withhold important evidence that would call the aims and plans into question. I'll give you two examples of groupthink in a moment.

5. **Focus on external enemies:** This can be a way of (a) preventing the team or group from splintering by creating a temporary unifying force centred on external dangers, real or imagined or of (b) living out the team's story. For example, executive teams focusing on competitors. Or top sports teams complaining about referees, clashing with governing bodies and lashing out at journalists. This can hold teams together for a while, but if members continue focusing on external imaginary enemies they may become paranoid, drain their energy and lose sight of their original aims. It may also lead to denial, cover-ups (remember FIFA and the Roman Catholic Church) and lethal actions (think again of lynch mobs killing the targets of their hate and anger because their story justifies their actions). There's another risk: gripped by paranoia, an executive team's idea of "enemies" may widen to include other departments in its parent company, reducing cooperation and harming overall results.

6. **Collective fragility under pressure:** This stems from a team's shared belief in a powerful negative "story" about its collective capability, often magnified by an absence of shared values or long-term purpose that might have brought deep meaning and motivation to its members. How it shows in action depends on the team's line of work. But talented performers who do well in other conditions can crumble under the fear the Collective "story" force creates and execute poorly when facing challenges they fear most. I believe past England football teams have displayed this effect.

Clients usually recognise five of the six patterns, but most aren't familiar with number four, "groupthink". Irving Janis coined the term to describe cases where group members are so concerned with preserving harmony and ducking conflict they avoid critical analysis, overlook important facts and opinions, rely on false assumptions and agree foolish plans.

A famous example of groupthink was the Bay of Pigs fiasco in 1961. The US government led by the recently elected President Kennedy and some Cuban exiles tried to launch a counter-revolution to Fidel Castro's communist takeover two years earlier. Janis' research revealed that some of Kennedy's advisers had serious doubts but didn't voice them. Others withheld important data or suppressed opinions that could have changed the goal or the plan or perhaps stopped the idea in its tracks. The result? A humiliating failure with most of the invading force killed or captured. But take note: the advisers around President Kennedy weren't feeble fools. They were strong able men, but the Collective group survival force, expressing in this case as groupthink, overpowered them by making unity the overriding priority.[36]

The Royal Bank of Scotland's (RBS) takeover of ABN-Amro in October 2007 was a business example of groupthink. It sent RBS into financial meltdown seven months later. In early 2007, the RBS board had committed itself to organic growth rather than chasing expensive takeovers. Yet only three months later not one board member formally expressed doubts about the wisdom of buying ABN-Amro because staying united was the subconscious priority. Four years on, *The Failure of the Royal Bank of Scotland*, the Financial Service Authority's official 2011 report into the RBS debacle, referred to groupthink at board level as one key reason it happened.[37]

Collective forces summary

To summarise, Collective forces appear when teams and groups develop a shared identity, purpose, values, and sense of capability that spawns shared norms, opinions and behaviours. From all this, living systems emerge that want to survive and enact their "story".

When teams and work groups feel under pressure, the survival drive (the second Collective force) or the negative story (the first Collective force) start affecting their unwitting creators.

In teams and small work groups, Collective forces show in six specific ways: (1) leader over-dependency (2) leader scapegoating (3) a focus on external enemies (4) avoidance of issues (5) groupthink and (6) collective fragility. All six have unhelpful effects on teams' performance under pressure. I've illustrated this in figure 4.

Figure 4: Collective Forces & Behavioural Results

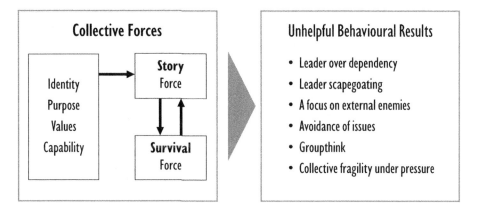

Individual Forces

The Collective forces are joint creations but the Individual forces flow separately from each member's subconscious beliefs. To be more exact, they flow from three types of beliefs – *worldview* beliefs, *self-image* beliefs and certain *values*. (Values are just a special class of beliefs). To be more accurate still, from specific *limiting* worldview beliefs, *limiting* self-image beliefs and certain *limiting* values. They are the three Individual forces. They cause unhelpful emotions and behaviour, increasing the complexity and challenge of working in teams. You will see this depicted in figure 5.

Because beliefs are the root of Individual forces it's worth understanding what they are and why we hold them before explaining *limiting* beliefs. Beliefs are simply ideas that we judge to be true and – in the case of values – guide what we think is important in life. Here's a closer look at the three types:

Figure 5: Components of Individual Forces

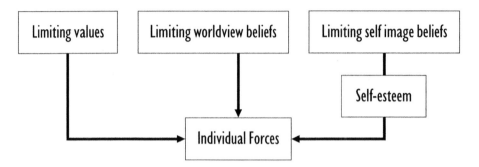

- *Values* are the special class of beliefs that motivate you most. They are your judgement of what matters in your life ... what you care about most. An example of a value would be, "Personal growth; the feeling that I'm always growing." In the context of Individual forces, there are three "value zones" that interest us: (1) conscientiousness (2) organisational citizenship and (3) individualism. We'll examine them shortly.
- *Worldview* beliefs summarise your understanding of the purpose of life, how life works and other people's motives. For example, "There is a God" or "There isn't a God, life has no inherent purpose" or "You can't trust anybody" or "What goes around comes around" or "Life is survival of the fittest." As with values, there are three worldview zones that concern us here: (1) your trust in others' motives (2) your belief in their commitment to doing the best job possible and (3) your attitude to people above you in the hierarchy.
- *Self-image* (or self-identity) beliefs are ideas about who you are: your qualities, your flaws, your potential and your place in the world. You define your self-image in the words that follow "I am...". Three specific self-image beliefs have the greatest effect on Individual forces: (1) your belief in your innate significance (2) your belief in your abilities and judgement, and (3) your belief in your likeability. These beliefs control your self-esteem. How so? Because "self-esteem" is simply the sum total of your feelings

about your self-image. So if your self-image is negative, you'll feel badly about yourself.

Why do we hold beliefs? Because we often need them, which makes them helpful. After all, we can't experience everything life has to offer, so we use beliefs to motivate and guide us through situations where we lack personal experience. In this way, beliefs act as useful proxies for truth. For example, I don't know from personal experience that it's dangerous to provoke a King Cobra, the world's biggest venomous snake. But I believe it's true. And I judge it to be a helpful belief as it ensures I don't put myself at unnecessary risk.

But not all of our beliefs are true or helpful.

Limiting beliefs, which account for two of the three classes of Individual forces, are neither true nor helpful. They are negative subconscious ideas we have about our character, abilities, life, and other people that we assume are true.

Worldview limiting belief force

In my experience, three common worldview limiting beliefs make up the first Individual force affecting people working in teams and small groups:

The key worldview limiting beliefs	• "Others don't share my standards of workmanship; they'll let me down." • "You can't trust anybody; they'll only take advantage of you." • "People in power have special privileges; I mustn't challenge them."

How do they affect people's contribution in teams? They cause them to behave defensively to avoid certain fears. For example, a belief like "You can't trust anybody; they'll take advantage of you" can make us reluctant to say what we're really thinking and feeling for fear of being manipulated, hurt, rejected, punished or ostracised.

Similarly, the belief that "Others don't share my standards of workmanship, they'll only let me down" can mean leaders reject colleagues' help even when they need it. Or it can mean they refuse to delegate because they're afraid others will make mistakes, leading to failures.

And those who believe "People in power have special privileges, we mustn't challenge them" can refuse to use their initiative or under-contribute without instructions from senior figures because they believe they don't have the right to act or they fear criticism from above.[38]

You'll see these effects among figure 6's complete list of unhelpful Individual behaviours. Figure 6 appears at the end of this section on Individual forces.

Self-image limiting belief force

I've found these (or slight variations around them) are the three most common self-image limiting beliefs affecting people's behaviour in teams:

The key self-image limiting beliefs	• "I'm insignificant; no one's interested in my opinion here." • "I'm not good enough; I'll only fail or make mistakes." • "I'm unlikeable; no one will ever trust me or feel close to me."

This second Individual category has a huge influence over our thoughts, feelings and actions in teams, but its mechanism is more subtle than the worldview beliefs. Why? Mainly because we're so identified with our self-image limiting beliefs that it doesn't occur to us they're anything other than the truth.

Putting it another way, we identify so closely *with* a belief like "I'm not good enough" that we identify ourselves *as* the belief. In this way, our self-image limiting beliefs form powerful filters controlling our self-esteem and confirming everything we experience. The harsh reality is this: the limiting beliefs we unconsciously identify with direct many of our choices, thinking patterns, emotional reactions, behavioural habits and relationships. It's not too strong to say they rule our lives. How? Through shame and fear. I'll explain...

Negative self-image beliefs like "I'm not good enough" and "I'm insignif-icant" lower our self-esteem and induce pain: the pain of shame. Shame isn't the same as guilt. We feel guilt when we judge we've done something wrong or failed to do something important. In other words, guilt is driven by action (or inaction). But shame is different in two ways. First, it's more powerful and more toxic than guilt. Second, it stems not from what we've done or failed to do, but from who we think we are – our self-identity or self-image. We don't have the space here for an in-depth look at shame and its origins, but if you'd like to know more, try reading the section on guilt and shame in my earlier book, The Three Levels of Leadership. The point is that shame hurts. Indeed, it hurts so much that most of us push it so far into our subconscious mind that we become unaware of it.

Unfortunately that's no escape because shame produces fear. For example, if we believe we're not good enough, we'll be afraid of failing or making a mistake or admitting there's something we don't know or understand. Why do these possibilities feel so bad? Because we fear the humiliation we assume these experiences will bring. If instead we think we're unlikable we fear rejection by our colleagues if we say what we're really thinking or feeling. And if we believe we're insignificant, what do we fear most? Being ignored. Why? Because that will only confirm what we already "knew" (or rather believed) – that we're a nobody. And that will remind us of our shame.

The combination of shame and fear is so unpleasant we find ways of avoiding the potential threat so we create subconscious defence mechanisms: thinking, feeling and behavioural habits designed to ensure we don't meet the conditions we're most afraid of. Unfortunately the defences often show as unhelpful behaviour in teams – behaviour that blocks the team's success.[39] I've listed examples in figure 6. They include sullen body language, repeatedly missing or turning up late for meetings, hidden agendas, "elephants in the room" and other problems.

Limiting values force

Values define what matters to us in choosing priorities and actions.

We hold values in many areas of our lives, but from the angle of unhelpful behaviour in teams, research highlights three values of interest:[40]

Key Limiting Values	Associated Beliefs
Low conscientiousness	"It's not important to give my best in every task I undertake; I don't care about doing tasks well or on time."
Low organisational citizenship	"I'll do what I'm paid to do and that's it; I've no interest in helping the company over and above my specific job duties."
Individualism over collectivism	"My priorities are more important than the team's – if I have to make a choice, I'll always look after number one first."

All three values, individually or together, can cause an unhelpful effect called "social loafing". I've included it among the behaviours listed in figure 6. "Social loafing" is where individuals contribute less work in a team than they would working solo, meaning the team's results are below the combined potential of its members: the 2+2 = 3 effect. Loafing members tell themselves, "We have enough people here to do the job, I'll let them do the work and take a backseat." Social loafing is common. I've done it and I'll bet you have too. Endnote 41 offers more detail on social loafing if you're interested.

To be clear, Individual forces are not the sole drivers of social loafing, but the three values I've just listed are among its chief causes.[41] Not surprisingly, when people don't value conscientiousness, social loafing is more likely. And when people's interest in organisational citizenship is low – typified by the "I've no interest in helping the company over and above my specific job duties" value – you're also more likely to see social loafing. Finally, when people stress personal achievement, satisfaction and happiness over the team's success, again, research shows social loafing is more likely.

Individual forces summary

To bring everything together in this section on Individual forces, figure 6 shows examples of the common Individual-driven behaviours and problems you'll see in teams.[42] The behaviours I've listed are widespread. They are not extreme, rare or unusual. I suspect you'll have seen all of them at some time. There's a good chance you've committed some of them.

Figure 6: Individual Forces & Behavioural Results

Team Members' Individual Forces

Key Worldview Beliefs

"Others don't share my high standards; they'll only let me down."

"You can't trust anybody; they'll only take advantage of you

"I mustn't challenge the authority of people in power."

Key Self Image Beliefs

"I am not good enough; I'll fail or make mistakes."

"I am unlikeable; no one will like or trust me."

"I am insignificant they won't listen to me."

Key Values

"I don't care about doing tasks well or on time."

"I'll do what I'm paid to do and that's it; I won't help the company over and above my specific job duties."

"My priorities matter more than the team's I'll always look after number one first."

Unhelpful Behavioural Results

- Leaders under delegating / micromanaging
- Leaders rejecting colleagues' help
- Members not saying what they're really thinking and feeling (elephant in the room).
- Social loafing or refusing to take the initiative.
- Repeatedly avoiding meetings.
- Repeatedly turning up late for meetings.
- Repeatedly not speaking up at meetings.
- Hidden agendas.
- Sullen body language.
- Pairing up / cliques.
- Repeated finger pointing.
- Power struggles.
- Leaders crushing opposition or debate.
- Leaders avoiding responsibilities.
- Saying one thing but doing another (sabotage)
- Members not delivering on their promises.

These behaviours aren't always created by Individual forces. Other influences like poor chairing of meetings or an uninspiring team purpose can also drive them. But singly or combined, the left-hand panel's beliefs and values can cause all sixteen behaviours in the right-hand panel. All we need to grasp here are the many problems Individual forces can cause. If you wish to see the specific link between each behaviour and its controlling Individual forces, you'll find the detail in endnote 43.[43]

All 16 defensive behaviours in figure 6 are immediately clear except perhaps one: *executive sabotage*. Have you attended meetings where you thought you'd reached a team decision to follow a certain path or complete certain actions ... and then, strangely, nothing happens ... or it's poorly executed ... and the decision unravels, but no one understands why? Most executives have. Why and how does that happen? Usually it's because team members have either pretended to agree to something or not admitted they disagree, but after the meeting they've started grumbling and politicking in corridors and private offices, unpicking the original decision. Or instead of behind-the-scenes politicking, senior executives will signal their apathy or dissent to their staff by mocking the plan verbally or through more subtle body language (for example, rolling their eyes) or giving the project a low priority, leading to low-energy, sloppy follow-through. All this is what I call "executive sabotage".

The point is that Individual forces can and do create at least sixteen unhelpful behaviours that make life in teams and small work groups more difficult. If you ignore them, they'll block a team's success.

The Emotional Combustion Chamber

What happens when the Collective and Individual forces combine to exert pressure on team members? They create the "emotional combustion chamber" illustrated in figure 7.

You'll find combustion chambers in petrol, diesel and jet engines. They're where fuel and air are mixed, put under pressure and ignited to create the controlled continuous explosions that propel cars and jets forward. Controlled explosions are, of course, what you want in cars and jets. But teams don't set out to create such fiery conditions. However, that's what unbridled interplay of Collective and Individual forces will produce.

Figure 7: Emotional Combustion Chamber in Teams

Individual Forces

Collective Forces

- Team story
- Team survival

Individual Forces

- Individual limiting values
- Individual worldview limiting beliefs
- Individual self image limiting beliefs

Team members' operating space becomes an "emotional combustion chamber"

By using the "emotional combustion chamber" metaphor I'm not suggesting teams are always on the point of exploding. But I am saying the two forces' combined effect can produce charged atmospheres with hidden undercurrents and agendas that confuse, discourage or demotivate team members. Hence my earlier metaphor of snooker balls cannoning into one another. That's when misunderstandings occur and get-togethers become boring, frustrating and fruitless or, alternatively, tense and unpleasant.

The ultimate effect on the team's performance? You'll see five possibilities, all unwanted:

- Important decisions avoided.
- Poor decisions made.
- Low creativity.
- Excessive or insufficient risk-taking.
- Poor execution, especially under pressure.

There's one more potential result. If it's the top team, its behaviour will set a bad example to others, damaging morale, lowering standards and slowing (or blocking) progress.

Conclusion

The psychological detail in this appendix is helpful, but you don't have to remember it all, just the overall message: *that teams exert powerful socio-psychological forces on us as members, making it harder to work together.* Thus, groups don't become teams by accident. It takes insight, skill, effort, time and practice to sidestep the negative Individual and Collective forces and create a cohesive, strong-willed, creative team that doesn't buckle under pressure. Helping you to gain this insight and skill is the aim of How To Build Winning Teams Again and Again.

The Key Points...

- Most people find it harder to express themselves in teams than when they work one-to-one. The reason? Working in groups creates anxiety.

- Over the last one hundred years researchers and thinkers have tried to describe what happens in groups and why things become difficult. If you try studying their many writings, much of it expressed in psychotherapeutic language, you'll probably feel confused. So I've created a model that integrates and simplifies what they have to tell us: the Dual Forces model. In this model, I've described two forces that affect us in teams: *Collective* forces and *Individual* forces.

- Collective forces stem from the living system created jointly by the team members without them realising.

- Individual forces flow out from each team member's mind and collide with the forces flowing from their teammates.

- More detail on the Collective forces:

- Collective forces develop when a group gains an identity, a purpose, a set of values and a sense of its ability. From this, a living system emerges. Living systems want to survive and live out their stories. The identity-purpose-values-capability *story* is the first Collective force and the *survival drive* is the second. Both sub-forces influence what team members think, feel and do under pressure.

- Although the members create the Collective forces, usually without realising, they take on a life of their own. In this way they can cause living systems to behave like Doctor Frankenstein's monster, meaning the forces oppress the members, making them conform to the story and need to survive.

- The second Collective force – the *team's survival drive* – can in extreme cases, such as the Roman Catholic Church and FIFA scandals, push individual members to behave illegally or immorally in the face of an external threat and do things they wouldn't do outside the team.

- The same is true of the first Collective force – the *team's story*. The difference is that it doesn't stem from an outside threat to the team's survival. Also, their immoral behaviour may be less widely spread but more extreme (it may even extend to killing people). I offered the general example of lynch mobs and the specific case of the Mountain Meadow massacre.

- The team's *story* can have another unwanted effect: it can cause members to perform well below their potential under pressure if they doubt their collective capability, lack a clear motivating purpose or don't have powerful supporting values. However, in certain cases a team's story can have helpful effects. I gave you the example of the

New Zealand All Blacks post-2003. Crafting a positive story is one piece of the 7P team building model in Book Two of *How To Build Winning Teams Again and Again*.

- In executive, project and sports teams you'll often see the survival and story forces expressed in six ways when members feel fearful – perhaps because results are poor or they're tackling a high-risk, high-stakes project or they face external criticism. They are:

  1. Leader over-dependency.
  2. Leader scapegoating.
  3. Avoidance of issues.
  4. Groupthink.
  5. Focus on external enemies.
  6. Collective fragility.

- More detail on the Individual forces:

  - Individual forces flow from members' personal beliefs and values. More specifically, nine *limiting values* and *beliefs* create the Individual forces that trigger unhelpful behaviours. The limiting beliefs stem from individual members' self-images or worldviews. The values concern conscientiousness, organisational citizenship and individualism.

  - Limiting self-image beliefs lower our self-esteem, making us prey to shame and fear, causing defensive behaviours. Thus, members' self-esteem has a huge effect on the life of teams and small work groups.

  - Singly or combined, these limiting beliefs and values can cause sixteen unhelpful behaviours:

    1. Leaders under-delegating, over-controlling or micromanaging.
    2. Leaders rejecting help even when they need it.
    3. Members not saying what they're really thinking or feeling.

4. Refusing to use our initiative and creativity OR social loafing.
5. Repeatedly avoiding meetings.
6. Repeatedly turning up late for meetings.
7. Repeatedly not speaking up at meetings.
8. Working to hidden agendas (concealed clashing motives).
9. Sullen body language.
10. Pairing up and cliques.
11. Repeated finger-pointing.
12. Power struggles.
13. Leaders crushing opposition or debate.
14. Leaders ducking responsibilities, e.g. decisions or removal of team members.
15. Saying one thing but doing another, what I call "executive sabotage".
16. Not delivering on promises.

- Combined, the Collective and Individual forces create an emotional combustion chamber, triggering hidden undercurrents and agendas and chaotic behaviour. This only confuses, discourages or demotivates team members. The likely results?

1. Unproductive and perhaps unpleasant meetings.
2. Members avoiding key decisions or instead making poor choices.
3. Members losing their collective ability to solve big problems with fresh thinking.
4. Sloppy execution of decisions or collective underperformance under pressure.
5. Reckless risk-taking or its opposite, too little creative risk-taking.
6. Top teams setting a bad example, damaging company morale and results.

- You needn't remember every idea in this appendix, just one thought: *groups won't become real teams if you allow the Collective and Individual forces to run riot.* Putting it another way, groups don't become teams by accident. It takes insight, time and conscious effort to weaken or avoid the dual forces and build cohesive, strong-willed, creative teams that endure.

Notes

Chapter 1: This Pathway & Its Payoffs

[1] "It's not rocket science" (page 13)

Admittedly, if you keep talking to them you'll find out that although rocket science is relatively straightforward (assuming you've grasped the physics), rocket engineering, that is, designing and building rockets and all their interconnecting systems, is complex. Look for example at the problems NASA had with Apollo 13.

[2] Sir Alex Feguson and Pep Guardiola (page 14)

Sir Alex Feguson was the manager of Manchester United football club from 1986 to 2013 and in that time he led a succession of teams to 38 trophies. In his previous roles at Aberdeen and St Mirren his teams won another 12 trophies making 50 in all. Sir Alex is the most successful manager in the history of professional football.

Pep Guardiola has managed Barcelona, Bayern Munich and Manchester City over the last 14 years (it's now late 2022). In that time his teams have won 30 trophies.

[3] "75% of cross-functional teams fail" (page 14)

The article was *75% of Cross Functional Teams Are Dysfunctional* (Behnam Tabrizi, Harvard Business Review, 23 June 2015).

[4] "Others have reported similarly dismal findings." (page 14)

In her Human Resource Executive Online article, *Why Teams Fail – and What to Do About It*, Eunice Parisi-Carew reported that 60% of work teams fail.

Chapter 2: A Work Group in Turmoil

[5] Sources for the Handforth Council story

- *Handforth residents slam behaviour of parish councillors:* Knutsford Guardian, Monday, 15 May 2017.
- *Insults and expletives turn parish council Zoom meeting into internet sensation:* The Guardian, Friday 5 February 2021.
- *Handforth parish council: the history of a feud:* The Independent, Friday 5 February 2021.
- *Handforth Parish Council warned over election blocking and misconduct claims:* Chester Chronicle, Friday 5 February 2021.
- *Handforth Parish Council are not fit for purpose:* Wilmslow.co.uk, Friday, 5 February 2021
- *This 17-year-old sent Handforth Parish Council and Jackie Weaver viral:* The Manc, Saturday 6 February 2021.
- *Parish council that went viral over committee meeting is subject of "multiplicity of complaints":* Local Government Lawyer, Monday 8 February 2021.
- *Handforth Parish Council – No-confidence vote after Zoom meeting:* BBC News, Wednesday 10 February 2021.
- *You Have No Authority Here – What Happened at the Handforth Parish Council Meeting:* The Verdict, Wednesday 3 March 2021.

- *Two Handforth parish council members quit after viral Zoom call:* The Guardian, Thursday, 29 April 2021.
- Minutes of the extraordinary meeting of the Handforth Parish Council planning and environment committee held on Thursday, 10 December 2020 at 7:00pm. https://handforthtowncouncil.gov.uk/
- Minutes of the extraordinary meeting of Handforth Parish Council held on Thursday 10 December 2020 at 7:30pm. https://handforthtowncouncil.gov.uk/
- Handforth Town Council statement issued by John Smith, council chair, sometime after July 2021. https://handforthtowncouncil.gov.uk/
- Roles & Responsibilities of Town Council Personnel: http://www.nelsontowncouncil.gov.uk
- Wikipedia page for Handforth Town Council: https://en.wikipedia.org/wiki/Handforth Town Council
- YouTube video: The Prequel to the Extraordinary Meeting of the Handforth Parish Council: https://www.youtube.com/watch?v=yCSQ4taJ-so
- YouTube video: Full Video of the Extraordinary Meeting of the Handforth Parish Council: https://www.youtube.com/watch?v=cNVcDDW1Hrs

Chapter 3: It Takes Effort to Create Teams

[6] "Research shows that 75% of teams fail" (page 30)

Behnam Tabrizi reported this finding in his 2015 Harvard Business Review article, *"75% of Cross Functional Teams Are Dysfunctional"*. He studied 95 teams in 25 leading companies, chosen by an independent panel of academics and experts. In fact, they weren't just dysfunctional, they failed. More specifically, they failed on at least three of five criteria: (1) meeting a planned budget (2) staying on schedule (3) adhering to specifications (4) meeting customer expectations (5) maintaining alignment with the company's corporate goals. His article was published in Harvard Business Review on 23 June 2015.

[7] Unhelpful defensive behaviours (page 42)

In describing the effects of self-image and worldview beliefs I've referred to "defensive behaviours". To be clear, behaviours are only defensive when three conditions are true. One, we use them repeatedly even when they're not our wisest option and behaving differently would be smarter for us and colleagues. In other words, we overuse them. Two, the unconscious motive behind them is to prevent us experiencing our fears. Three, we don't choose them; they are habits we find hard to break.

[8] The three values that may cause problem behaviours in teams and groups (page 43)

Tan & Tan's 2008 study, *Organizational Citizenship Behavior and Social Loafing: The Role of Personality, Motives and Contextual Factors*, found that less conscientious people are more likely to engage in social loafing. It was their study that also showed a correlation between a weak sense of responsibility beyond one's contractual job duties (low organisational citizenship) and social loafing. Not surprisingly, they noted a correlation between conscientiousness and organisational citizenship as although they are distinct, they're not entirely separate.

The importance of the individualism-versus-collectivism value was confirmed by Klehe and Anderson in their 2007 study, *The Moderating Influence of Personality and Culture on Social Loafing in Typical Versus Maximum Performance Situations*. It showed that people from individualistic cultures (e.g. North America, Western Europe) are more likely to loaf than those in collectivist cultures (e.g. Far East, Latin America), where group goals are considered more important than individual success.

[9] Individual forces and unhelpful group behaviours (page 44)

Here I'm drawing heavily, but not exclusively, on the work of William Schutz, the originator of FIRO theory, for the ideas around self-image limiting beliefs. Schutz first outlined his theory in 1958 in his first book, *FIRO: A Three-Dimensional Theory of Interpersonal Behavior*. He refined the theory in his 1994 book, *The Human Element: Productivity, Self-Esteem and the Bottom Line*. Where I am not drawing on Schutz, I'm either using the research into social loafing by Max Ringelmann, Alan Ingham et al, Tan & Tan, and Klehe & Anderson (their papers are listed in the bibliography) or relying on my own executive coaching experience (which has highlighted the presence of worldview limiting beliefs).

Chapter 4: The Team Progression Curve

[10] Team progression curve (page 52)

This model is a synthesis of the research and ideas of Katzenbach & Smith (*The Wisdom of Teams*, 1993) and William Schutz (*Profound Simplicity*, 1979 and *The Human Element*, 1994) plus the writings of Jarlath Benson (*Working More Creatively with Groups*, 2001) and David Whitaker (*The Spirit of Teams*, 1999), together with my own insights into and experience of teams. I believe the underlying theory and labels proposed by William Schutz around groups' developmental issues and, to some degree the phases they go through, don't quite fit the evolution of a team, which is a specific kind of group. I have therefore built on and modified his theory, creating the "three Cs" of Commit-Combust-Combine, which apply specifically to teams.

[11] The Wisdom of Teams by Katzenbach & Smith (page 53)

Jon Katzenbach and Douglas Smith studied 47 executive teams and published their landmark research in the excellent book, *The Wisdom of Teams* (1993). Anyone interested in teams should read it. Their follow-up book was *The Discipline of Teams* (2001).

They were the first to distinguish between what they called "working groups" and teams. My "performance groups" and their "working groups" are identical. I chose not to use their "working group" label because it would be confusing as I've used the term "work groups" as an umbrella term to cover performance groups, task groups and teams. Katzenbach and Smith didn't recognise task groups as a separate category, but observation and experience tells me they are different so it's right to separate them out from performance groups.

[12] Intrinsic motivators (page 54)

There are two forms of motivation: extrinsic and intrinsic.

Extrinsic motivation relies on external pressures and rewards, including incentives and punishments (or the threat of punishment), to move people towards a target behaviour and, beyond that, a certain result. Some people call it "carrot and stick" motivation.

Intrinsic motivation doesn't rely on external pressures. With intrinsic motivation we feel inspired to exert effort because the activity is so interesting, challenging, creative or fulfilling that we don't need an external prompt. Engaging in the activity is itself innately motivating.

What inspires intrinsic motivation? Research, mainly from Edward Deci and Richard Ryan (the founders of Self-Determination Theory), but also by Adam Grant, tells us there are four intrinsic motivators. They are: (1) autonomy (2) competence (3) purpose and (4) relatedness.

Autonomy is feeling that you can choose what work you do, how you do it, when you do it and with whom. *Competence* is feeling that you are continually learning, that you're getting better at your work or hobby, that you're mastering it, that you're growing. *Purpose* gives you the feeling that there's an important reason behind what you're doing, that you are making a worthwhile difference, one that benefits others (not just your selfish interests), which confers on you a sense of personal significance. *Relatedness* makes you feel your work is connected to others' efforts, that you're part of something bigger than you, that others have your back while you have theirs.

Real Teams are excellent vehicles for experiencing three of the four intrinsic motivators: competence, purpose and relatedness. If you wish to read more on intrinsic motivation, there is a section in my book The Three Levels of Leadership (second edition, 2016). You'll find it on pages 113–128.

[13] "Research shows that High-Performance Teams are rare" (page 54)

The term "high-performance team" (HPT) is often bandied about. It's used so casually that it's almost lost meaning. I find that when people talk about "high-performance teams" they are referring to what I call a "real team". But here, when I talk about HPTs, I'm using a definition first offered by Jon Katzenbach and Douglas Smith in *The Wisdom of Teams*.

The true high-performance team is distinguished, above all, by its members' exceptional dedication to one another. Supporting this are two other characteristics: (1) shared leadership and (2) the sense that, together, they are working towards a cause, not just a target, that's bigger than them.

During their research, Katzenbach & Smith found that HPTs are rare in organisations. Why? Because the commitment to team colleagues demanded in HPTs clashes with companies' cultural preference for individual over team accountability. If you look at people's job descriptions, bonus plans, career paths and performance evaluations, they almost always focus on individuals. Not only that, ask yourself this: are you comfortable entrusting your career hopes to results that depend on others' performance? Most people working in organisations aren't. Or they weren't when Katzenbach and Smith were conducting their research.

[14] "A ruthless 'top-down, do whatever it takes to hit the numbers' attitude is not a high-performance ethos" (page 59)

By way of contrast, this is what I'd call a high-pressure ethos. For a while it can gets results, but it can lead to burnout, division, "turf" protection, silos and "massaging" of financial results to make them look better than they really are.

[15] Less than 7% of teams studied were high-performance teams (page 60)

Once again, this is taken from Katzenbach and Smith's research, published in *The Wisdom of Teams*.

[16] Story about the high-performance basketball team (page 61)

This was told to me by Jerry Estenson, a professor at California State University, Sacramento, in a private email on 9 August 2016.

[17] Martin Murphy comment (page 62)

This was taken from a 1 October 2015 article by Martin Murphy on LinkedIn. You can find it at https://www.linkedin.com/pulse/what-being-sas-taught-me-leadership-teamwork-business-martin/

[18] Professor Estenson's comments on the "dark side" of high-performance teams (page 63)

Jerry Estenson described his experiences in an email to me on 9 August 2016.

Chapter 5: Performance Groups and Real Teams

[19] "Team leaders do real work" (page 73)

Again, this draws on Katzenbach and Smith's research findings in *The Wisdom of Teams* (1993).

Chapter 6: Why So Few Senior Teams?

[20] "Few so-called senior management teams are real teams" (page 84)

Data to support this point first came to light in Jon Katzenbach and Douglas Smith's landmark research for their book, *The Wisdom of Teams* (1993) where they studied 47 executive teams and, again, in their follow-up work in *The Discipline of Teams*, 2001. They commented in The Wisdom of Teams that, "there are fewer teams at the top of large organisations" (page 3). A later study by Wageman, Nunes, Burruss & Hackman published in their book *Senior Leadership Teams* (2008) lent support to this insight, but in a slightly different way. Of the 120 "top teams" they studied, 79% were rated mediocre or poor. I'd suggest this is because they weren't real teams. It's certainly my personal experience that few "senior teams" are real teams. The ones I've seen are nearly always performance groups.

[21] Roles that make members feel included and important (page 88)

I've commented that when team members feel they have distinct roles they feel included and important, which raises their motivation. See the research on social loafing, summarised in endnote 41, for more on this point.

Chapter 7: Seeing Through the Fog I: C-C-C (Overview)

[22] Group development models since the 1950s (page 96)

I am referring to three major pieces of research and theory development concerning the evolution of small groups.

The first is by William Schutz, who developed the *Inclusion-Control-Openness* model, which I've drawn on. Schutz's work wasn't specific to teams; it was based on a study of small groups in general. Schutz develop the I-C-O model as a subset of his influential Fundamental Interpersonal Relations Orientation (FIRO) theory in 1958 and updated it over the following 35 years. He originally called the third stage, Affection, but changed it to Openness in the early 1990s. I've drawn on his theory as expressed in his books, FIRO: *A Three-Dimensional Theory of Interpersonal Behavior* (1958), *The Human Element: Productivity, Self-Esteem and the Bottom Line* (1994) and *Profound Simplicity* (1979).

The second is by Bruce Tuckman. He is known for his *Forming-Storming-Norming-Performing* model, which was influenced by Schutz's prior work. It was published as a paper in Psychological Bulletin (1965) titled *Developmental Sequence in Small Groups*. His model is similar to Schutz's, but he adds a fourth stage, *Performing*, which is implied within Schutz's third stage. Crucially, he also gave his developmental process a more memorable set of labels. In practice, I doubt it's necessary to distinguish between the Norming and Performing stages, so I prefer the simpler classification, and I don't think they always happen in sequence. In 1977, Tuckman added a fifth stage, *Adjourning*, to mark the group's end phase.

The third is by Garland, Jones & Kolodny who proposed five stages in their 1965 paper: *A Model of Stages in the Development of Social Work Groups*. Their stages: *Pre-Affiliation, Power & Control, Intimacy, Differentiation and Separation.*

The Schutz, Tuckman and Garland models overlap, especially around the connection/belonging, power/control and affection/closeness/intimacy sequence, which is reassuring.

[23] Bruce Tuckman's "Form-Storm-Norm-Perform" model (page 96)

Tuckman was working at the Naval Medical Research Institute in the USA. His model appeared as an article in Psychological Bulletin titled *Developmental Sequence in Small Groups* in 1965 (volume 63, pp. 384–399). He added a fifth stage in 1977: "Adjourn". His model was a synthesis of 50 articles and books describing stages of group development over time, one of which was by William Schutz.

Many people overlook one important point when referring to Tuckman's work in relation to teams: few of the books and articles he drew on in creating his model reflected work groups, never mind teams. Most of the groups he studied were therapy groups (intended to help individuals deal with their personal problems better) and human relations training groups, sometimes called T-groups (where the aim was to develop interpersonal sensitivity).

[24] William Schutz's FIRO research and model (page 96)

I have drawn on William Schutz's research into groups in creating the Commit-Combust-Combine model. He first published his work as FIRO: *A Three-Dimensional Theory of Interpersonal Behavior* (Rinehart, New York, 1958). He refined and expanded his theory over the next 25 years before writing *The Human Element: Productivity, Self-Esteem and the Bottom Line* (Jossey-Bass, San Francisco, 1994).

His theory – which he developed for groups in general – not performance teams – has three phases: Inclusion, Control and Openness. His research revealed that groups first address belonging needs, then power needs and only then do they deal with their affection needs by focusing on closeness. The Commit-Combust-Combine model accepts this sequence but adapts the I-C-O theory to teams. This results in three differences.

Commit differs from *Inclusion* in two ways. First, the act of selecting members is an important part of Commit, but not of Inclusion. In business and in sport, team members don't join just because they want to, like the way they would join a social group or social club. Unlike Schutz's FIRO theory – which tried to explain all groups not just work groups – they don't decide the question of membership. Someone else puts them in the team. Perhaps a selection board. Or perhaps the team manager picks them. Or perhaps they are automatically in the team because they report to the leader. The point is, physical inclusion isn't their decision. They might want to be a team member, but the final decision isn't theirs. However – and this takes us to the second difference – members do control their mental and emotional commitment as in business and sports teams it's possible to be physically present (included), but not committed. So the second difference is that Schutz's Inclusion focuses more on the member's choice to physically join or not join a group, but in Commit we're more interested in members' inner commitment to playing a full part in achieving the team's purpose.

The third difference is between *Combine* and *Openness*. Schutz's Openness phase is all about openness, that is, members saying what they're really thinking and feeling, resulting in honesty, closeness, affection and development of trust. Combine accepts that openness is crucial but says it's not enough to produce a real team. There must also be team-wide commitment to the overall performance goal, with each person seeing the objective as both collective and personal. People not only say what they're really thinking and feeling, they follow through on their statements and promises. This ensures that members direct their growing intimacy and trust towards joint accountability and therefore to performance. After all, the team's raison d'être isn't cosy relations – it is there to deliver a result.

[25] William Schutz wheel analogy (page 106)

William Schutz described this useful analogy on page 114 of his book Profound Simplicity (*Profound Simplicity: Foundations for a Social Philosophy, fifth edition*, 2002).

[26] "Several pieces of research suggest you can't avoid these issues" (page 114)

These are the pieces of research by William Schutz, Bruce Tuckman and Garland, Jones & Kolodny that I referred to in note 22.

Chapter 8: Seeing Through The Fog II: C-C-C (Detail)

[27] Meredith Belbin's research into team roles (page 121)

This was research first conducted in the 1970s in the UK. Dr Belbin has written several books, but his seminal research was first published in *Management Teams: Why They Succeed or Fail* (Butterworth Heinemann, Oxford, 1981).

[28] Under-social and over-social behaviour (page 127)

These are terms William Schutz used in his book, *The Human Element: Productivity, Self-Esteem and the Bottom Line* (Jossey-Bass, 1994). I haven't found them used anywhere else.

Chapter 9: Seeing Through the Fog III: Evolution & Endings

[29] Problems with endings (page 167)

My main source for these comments was Jarlath Benson's book, *Working More Creatively with Groups* (second edition, 2001 published by Routledge), in particular, his chapter 7: "Work at the Ending Stage of the Group: Separation Issues". I also found this article by Joann Keyton useful: *Group Termination*, published in Small Group Research, February 1993.

Appendix: The Hidden Psychology of Teams

[30] Types of work groups (page 173)

I offered a full explanation of the differences between task groups, performance groups and real teams in chapter 4 of How To Build Winning Teams Again and Again.

[31] Group/team researchers and theorists (page 176)

I mentioned Wilfred Bion, William Schutz, Irving Janis and Gustave Le Bon in the text. In my view, the other key people in this field are Kurt Lewin, Robert Bales, Bruce Tuckman, Meredith Belbin, Roy Lacoursiere, and Max Ringelmann. A few brief comments:

- *Wilfred Bion:* Try Margaret Rioch's article: Rioch, M.J. (1970), The Work of Wilfred Bion on Groups published in the Journal for the Study of Interpersonal Processes (1970, Vol 33, Issue 1, pp 56–66). Bion described his ideas in a set of papers he wrote in the late 1940s. He combined them into a book titled Experiences in Groups, published in 1961.
- *William Schutz:* Schutz first outlined his theory in 1958 in his first book, FIRO: A Three-Dimensional Theory of Interpersonal Behavior. He refined the theory in his 1994 book, The Human Element: Productivity, Self-Esteem and the Bottom Line.
- *Irving Janis:* His 1982 landmark book was Groupthink: Psychological Studies of Polities Decisions and Fiascoes (second edition).
- *Gustave Le Bon:* He expressed his ideas in the late nineteenth century in The Crowd: A Study of the Popular Mind (1895).
- *Kurt Lewin:* there is no one key book or article. You could try Resolving Social Conflicts, which is a book containing selected papers on group dynamics. Lewin is seen as the father of "group dynamics".
- *Robert Bales:* working in the 1950s, Bales was the first to sift what happened in groups into task-orientated and relationship-orientated behaviours.
- *Bruce Tuckman:* wrote his classic article Developmental Sequences in Small Groups in 1965. It appeared in Psychological Bulletin, 63, 384–399.
- *Meredith Belbin:* his breakthrough book was Management Teams: Why They Succeed or Fail, 1981.
- *Roy Lacoursiere:* wrote The Life Cycle of Groups: Group Development Stage Theory in 1980.
- *Max Ringelmann:* was a French agricultural engineer. He discovered that individual members of groups often become increasingly less productive as the group's size increases. It became known as the Ringelmann effect. He published his findings in a French journal, Annales de l'Institut National Agronomique, in 1913.

[32] Crowd psychology and the overpowering of individual values (page 182)

I wrote in the main text "that groups and crowds can enable behaviour that individuals wouldn't commit or condone on their own." Support for this statement is provided by David Myers (*Psychology*, 10th edition, 2013, page 568) and Linda Geddes (*UK Riots: Why Respectable People Turned to Looting*, New

Scientist, 12 August 2011) who both commented on the riots that hit the UK's major cities in 2011.

Myers wrote: "During England's 2011 riots and looting, rioters were disinhibited by social arousal and the anonymity provided by darkness and their hoods and masks. Later, some of those arrested expressed bewilderment over their own behaviour."

Geddes wrote: "A millionaire's daughter, a school teaching assistant and a lifeguard are hardly the sort of people you'd have expected to get caught up in the wave of violent looting that hit the UK earlier this week. So what drives privileged or seemingly virtuous people to do bad things? ... As those responsible for the disturbances begin to appear in court, it is becoming clear that the looters were not all out-of-control teenagers with nothing to lose. They came from a variety of backgrounds and in some cases have expressed horror and regret at what they did."

Interviews with rioters backed up Myers and Geddes' comments:

- "Only 27% of the girls and women said they would take part in the riots if they happened again, compared with 37% of men and boys. Many of those interviewed, on reflection, felt their actions were wrong... A 42-year-old who handed herself into the police said: 'I felt guilty because I saw the aftermath. Some of the shops that had been hit we used, so we knew the owners,' she said. 'I felt pity for them. I saw the devastation of what happened. I didn't feel good about myself basically, so I thought it was the right thing to do.'... After the initial excitement had passed, one 16-year-old, who rioted in Clapham Junction and received looted goods, said she regretted the impact on the local community. 'It's stupid because now everyone's thinking, why did we actually do it? Like, you didn't really benefit from it; if anything we're just thinking, what did we do to where we live? You're basically breaking your own community.'" (*The Women Who Rioted*, article in The Guardian, 9 December 2011)
- "For others, there was a sense of personal regret. A 15-year-old girl described being scared and unwilling to take part when the riots flared up in her area. 'Then, after it all kicked off and everyone was doing it, you just joined in and it felt fine. It just felt natural, like you was just naturally shopping,' she said. But subsequently she handed herself in to the police, and, asked what she thought about her actions now, she said: 'I'm ashamed. To think that I went that low to go steal in these shops when they're, like, basically that's their business, that's how they're providing for their families, and we've basically ruined that and they've got to start from scratch.'" (*Reading The Riots: Investigating England's Summer of Disorder*, a report by The Guardian and London School of Economics & Political Science, December 2011)

Social psychologists offer three major theories for what happens when crowds act in ways that its members would normally consider wrong. (Note: there is a fourth crowd psychology theory, *Convergence*, but this doesn't explain the overpowering of individuals' values.

The first is Gustave Le Bon's *contagion* theory. Le Bon believed that people lose their self-awareness and sense of personal responsibility and self-restraint – a process that other social psychologists call deindividuation – when they find themselves in groups that arouse their feelings and allow anonymity. As individuals begin to act out their beliefs and emotions, actions become contagious and others follow until everyone's acting in concert – just like a disease spreading, only much faster. But as research by David Myers and George Bishop showed, their beliefs and actions don't just become contagious – often they become more intense and polarised through contact and discussion with like-minded people (*Discussion effects on racial attitudes*, Science, 21 August 1970, pp. 778–779).

The second is Henri Tajfel's *social identity* theory. The idea is that a group's identity, aims, moral and behavioural values, norms and standards play a role in defining its members' sense of identity and, as the group's purpose and values change, so the members' values and motives also change and dictate their collective action. But that's not all: groups that develop identity, purpose and values often divide the world into "them" – people outside our group – and "us". Tajfel used the labels "in-group" (us) and "out-group" (them). His theory says that in-group members will look for negative features of out-groups to criticise and discriminate against in order to boost their own self-image. At its worst, this can lead to prejudice, murder and genocide. We saw this in the Mountain Meadows massacre.

The third is Ralph Turner and Lewis Killian's *emergent norm* theory. It's the idea that norms emerge from within the crowd. They argued that crowds aren't united at the beginning, but as people talk, some suggest acting in a certain way and others fall in line. Thus, this assumes that leaders (or at least influential crowd members) emerge who shape the group's norms, which may override an individual's previously held values, especially once action starts, convincing some that "everyone can't be wrong".

Although it's not entirely accurate, you could say that what I describe as the Collective "story" force is an integration of these ideas. From this perspective, you could see the story force as starting with social identity and spreading through contagion, aided sometimes by deindividuation or the influence of emerging leaders.

[33] England football team's historical underperformance in tournament finals (page 183)

Analysts have suggested various explanations over the decades. For example: (1) "The players are tired at the end of a long season in which they haven't had a break, unlike other nations" (2) "They are poorly coached at youth level, leaving them with inferior technique" (3) "They are too paid too much, which makes them mentally soft."

These arguments don't stand up for two reasons. First, when the England players return to their clubs, their technique looks good and they don't exhibit the same frailty under pressure – it's only when they pull on an England shirt that their performances dip. Second, the Welsh national team made it through to the semi-finals of the 2016 European championships (still happening as I write this) and yet all three observations could be applied to them.

Most seasoned observers now believe that England teams down the years have suffered from a mental block at the finals – a collective psychological weakness under pressure. They think this is the key reason for England's continuing underperformance in tournament finals, culminating in their 2016 defeat by Iceland. Iceland has a population of 330,000 compared to England's 53 million and few of its players play for high-profile clubs outside Scandinavia. This combined with England's extraordinarily poor display led some experts to declare this to be England's worst ever result. An article by Liam Twomey on the ESPN website on 30 June 2016, just after England's defeat by Iceland, supported the view that England teams down the years have been suffering from a mental block that causes underperformance in times of high tension:

> Former England captain Steven Gerrard said in the Daily Telegraph that a "culture of fear" resulting from a history of failure is undermining the Three Lions at major tournaments. England suffered arguably their most humiliating defeat in a major tournament on Monday, losing 2–1 to Iceland in Nice to exit Euro 2016 at the round-of-16 stage...
>
> ... Gerrard, who captained England during two disappointing World Cups in 2010 and 2014, as well as at Euro 2012, believes the team will not improve as long as the players feel the weight of expectation and past disappointments.
>
> *"I do not accept that the problem with English football is that players are not good enough,"* Gerrard wrote in a column for the Daily Telegraph. *"It is the same argument whenever we go out of a major tournament. The players are overrated, and the English Premier League is not as strong as it thinks it is. Nonsense. You are telling me we do not have the talent to beat Iceland? That we lost because their players and their league are better than ours? We failed so badly on Monday night because of our poor decision-making, an inability to respond to events as they unfolded and because we repeated too many of the mistakes of the past."*
>
> England led inside four minutes in Nice when Wayne Rooney converted a penalty won by Raheem Sterling, but goals from Ragnar Sigurdsson and Kolbeinn Sigthorsson turned the tide before half-time in Nice. For much of the second half England were sluggish and uninspired, rarely threatening to score an equaliser, and Gerrard believes the players were dwelling on the potential fallout from losing to Iceland.

"When England went behind, many of those players will have been thinking of the consequences of defeat as much as what to do to get back in the game," Gerrard added. *"I hate to say it, but your mind drifts to what the coverage is going to be like back home and the level of criticism you are going to get. You cannot stop yourself: 'What if we don't get back into this? What will it be like if we go out here?' Panic sets in. The frustration takes over. You freeze and stop doing those things you know you should be. You start forcing the game, making the wrong choices with your passes, shooting from the wrong areas and letting the anxiety prevent you from doing the simple things. There is no environment of calm around the national team. There never has been. It is always hysteria. There is a culture of fear within and it has not been addressed."*

Many of England's players went into Euro 2016 fresh from excellent seasons at Premier League level, with the Tottenham Hotspur contingent having mounted the club's first genuine title challenge in years.

However, Gerrard says there is far greater pressure for players when representing the Three Lions. *"It is a different level to club football, where if you lose a big game there is usually never too long to get out there and make amends,"* he added. *"You can refocus quickly. With England, you know your chance is gone for another two years and the criticism will be ferocious. You know the eyes of the world are on you. The pressure is another level."*

Manchester City (and Belgium) captain, Vincent Kompany, agreed with Gerrard's assessment and says he didn't recognise the performances against Iceland as belonging to the players he regularly faces in the Premier League.

"I am shocked," Kompany, an ESPN analyst for Euro 2016, wrote in The Times. *"I wasn't expecting that. I thought that England would show their quality against Iceland, but what I saw was an extreme kind of collective failure. Looking from the outside, I honestly can't work out how it happened. What I do know is that when people respond by saying the players 'aren't good enough,' they are wrong. I have spent years playing against some of these players. You cannot tell me that the Harry Kane you see in the Premier League isn't good enough or that Raheem Sterling, Wayne Rooney, Joe Hart, Daniel Sturridge, Jack Wilshere, Chris Smalling and others 'aren't good enough.' These players are so much better than they appeared against Iceland. England had one of the strongest squads at Euro 2016 and yet something happened on Monday, a psychological 'event' to cause them to perform like that. It looked like something got to them."*

Source: https://www.espn.com/soccer/story/_/id/37477578/england-euro-2016-failure-result-culture-fear-steven-gerrard

Behind their psychological fragility (Gerrard's "culture of fear") is, I strongly suspect, a negative subconscious story that has grown over decades.

[34] New Zealand All Blacks rugby team and their positive "story" (page 184)

The New Zealand All Blacks are the world's leading rugby team in spite of a tiny population that only reached 4 million at the start of the 21st century. Until 2004, they had achieved a remarkable 75% win rate over the previous century. Despite that, they'd won the Rugby World Cup only once, in 1987. In 2004, after four failed World Cup campaigns, the All Blacks decided to press the reset button. They succeeded. Between 2004 and 2011 they pushed their win rate to an extraordinary 86%, lifting the 2011 World Cup along the way. They retained the World Cup in 2015.

How did they do it? As James Kerr explains in his book, *Legacy*, it wasn't a matter of tactics or fitness. Instead they consciously revisited and redefined their "story" to create a purpose-driven, values-based culture. They were already strong on "identity" and "capability" – the evidence is there in their previous 75% win record – but they fine-tuned their sense of "purpose" and "values". After 2004 they not only had answers to "who we are" and "what we're good at", they could now say what they stood for, why they existed and what it meant to be (and stay) an All Black. This became the source of competitive advantage. They defined their purpose as not simply winning matches or tournaments, but as leaving a legacy, "leaving the jersey in a better place". This gave greater significance to anyone becoming an All Black, raising individual motivation beyond simply winning the next game. To this they added values that brought the story to life like "train to win by practising under pressure", "no dickheads ... put character before ability when selecting players" and "no one is bigger than the team".

The All Blacks' "story" has served them well, which shows how helpful it is for teams to craft and reinforce a positive narrative over the years.

[35] How the Collective forces affect small work groups and teams (page 185)

This section draws on the work of Wilfred Bion, Irving Janis, Gustave Le Bon, Henri Tajfel and my own observation of sports teams and crowd behaviour. Bion identified the patterns of leader dependency, leader scapegoating, pairing (clique-forming) and a focus on outside enemies, although he used different, more opaque psychoanalytical language. He also referred to small groups' tendency to avoid conflict by ignoring issues, but it was Irving Janis who identified, studied and labelled the danger of groupthink. Gustave Le Bon was the first person to study crowds and offer a theory to explain their behaviour. Henry Tajfel was a social psychologist who studied prejudice and how group (social) identity affects both individual identity and intergroup relations.

Bion described his ideas in a set of papers he wrote in the late 1940s, which were later combined into a book titled *Experiences in Groups* (1961). Janis outlined his theory in his interesting readable book, *Groupthink* (1982). Le Bon expressed his ideas in the late nineteenth century in *The Crowd: A Study of the Popular Mind* (1895). Tajfel described his theory in a chapter of a book titled *The Social Identity Theory of Intergroup Behaviour*, which appeared in *Psychology of Intergroup Relations* (1986).

[36] Groupthink example #1: Bay of Pigs (page 188)

This case study was described in *Groupthink: Psychological Studies of Polities Decisions and Fiascoes* (second edition) by Irving Janis (1982).

[37] Groupthink example #2: Royal Bank of Scotland (page 188)

As described in *The Failure of the Royal Bank of Scotland*, a report by The Financial Services Authority Board in December 2011. The reference to "groupthink" is on page 229.

[38] Effect of "people in power have special privileges" belief (page 192)

This under-contribution is a form of social loafing.

[39] Unhelpful defensive behaviours (page 193)

In describing the effects of self-image and worldview beliefs I've referred to "defensive behaviours". To be clear, behaviours are only defensive when three conditions are true. One, we use them repeatedly even when they're not our wisest option and behaving differently would be smarter for us and colleagues. In other words, we overuse them. Two, the unconscious motive behind them is to prevent us experiencing our fears. Three, we don't choose them; they are habits we find hard to break.

[40] The three values that may cause problem behaviours in teams and groups (page 193)

Tan & Tan's 2008 study, *Organizational Citizenship Behavior and Social Loafing: The Role of Personality, Motives and Contextual Factors*, found that less conscientious people are more likely to engage in social loafing. It was their study that also showed a correlation between a weak sense of responsibility beyond one's contractual job duties (low organisational citizenship) and social loafing. Not surprisingly, they also found a correlation between conscientiousness and organisational citizenship as although they are distinct, they're not entirely separate.

The importance of the individualism-versus-collectivism value was confirmed by Klehe and Anderson in their 2007 study, *The Moderating Influence of Personality and Culture on Social Loafing in Typical Versus Maximum Performance Situations*. It showed that people from individualistic cultures (e.g. North America, Western Europe) are more likely to loaf than those in collectivist cultures (e.g.

Far East, Latin America), where group goals are considered more important than individual success.

[41] Social loafing (page 194)

Max Ringelmann discovered social loafing in an experiment in 1913. He asked participants to tug on a rope attached to a strain gauge measuring their pull strength. When only one person was pulling, participants averaged 63 kg of pressure. But when he asked two participants to pull they achieved only 117 kg, less than double the individual rate, which seemed strange. Even stranger, groups of three exerted a force of 160 kg, only 2.5 times the average individual performance, not three times as expected. For some reason, the individuals weren't trying so hard when they pulled together. Interestingly, when he experimented with a group of eight, they tried even less hard – they pulled at 248 kg, less than four times the individual rate. Putting it another way, pairs pulled at only 93% of the sum of the expected individual efforts, threesomes at 85% and groups of eight at only 49%.

Social psychologists ignored Ringelmann's work for over 50 years until, in 1974, four researchers (Alan Ingham et al) recreated the experiment and confirmed his results. They coined the term "social loafing". Other researchers have replicated Ringelmann's results many times as they explored its causes, effects and possible antidotes. They also confirmed that social loafing happens on both physical and cognitive tasks.

A helpful 2014 paper by Ashley Simms and Tommy Nichols, *Social Loafing: A Review of the Literature* provides an overview of all research so far into social loafing. Below is what it revealed about its probable causes and antidotes.

Causes: The causes aren't certain, but the numerous studies in this field have uncovered correlations between social loafing and various factors. Thus, we know the following factors make social loafing more likely:

- Low conscientiousness.
- Low organisational citizenship (zero interest in help your organisation beyond your contractual job duties).
- High individualism ("I'll always look after number one first; my priorities are far more important than the group's").
- Tasks that are judged unimportant by group members.
- Tasks that are judged boring or too easy by members.
- Tasks that members aren't skilled at.
- Individuals feeling that their contribution isn't needed, isn't noticed or isn't unique.
- Group members feeling low interdependence and cohesion.
- Members with low self-esteem needing validation of their "superiority" versus others.
- High respect for and obedience to people higher up (e.g. members believing that "people in power have special privileges and rights that I don't have so I mustn't challenge their instructions").
- Larger group size (meaning greater opportunity to be invisible).
- Members working on low-visibility tasks that offer little chance of recognition.
- Members who are habitually suspicious of others' motives and don't want to be taken as suckers by those who loaf (which causes a "loafing domino effect").
- An absence of performance feedback or performance-dependent rewards.

Antidotes: Not surprisingly, many of these are folded into the 7P model described in Book Two of *How To Build Winning Teams Again and Again* (chapters 12–19). Studies show that social loafing is less likely if these conditions are true:

- High group commitment to the task + a cohesive group + each person's input is identifiable + members' interactions produce a pressure to perform. (This is a multiple condition factor.)
- Group members' individual efforts are measured.
- The task is difficult, intrinsically interesting and one that members are skilled at.

- Members feel their individual contribution/role is unique.
- Members feel their individual contribution/role is visible.
- Individuals receive performance feedback on their contributions.
- There are performance-dependent rewards. (Note: but not non-performance-dependent rewards or punishment by authority figures).
- Members feel their tasks are interdependent (that they all rely on one another).
- Members feel their group task is important.
- Members are highly conscientious.
- Members value organisational citizenship (having a strong interest in helping their organisation over and above their contractual job duties).
- There is high collectivism, meaning members believe "the group's priorities come before my own."
- A low tendency to automatically obey people higher in the hierarchy plus a higher tendency to challenge their rules and ideas (known as "low power distance").

[42] Individual forces and unhelpful group behaviours (page 195)

Here I'm drawing heavily, but not exclusively, on the work of William Schutz, the originator of FIRO theory for the ideas around self-image limiting beliefs. Schutz first outlined his theory in 1958 in his book, FIRO: *A Three-Dimensional Theory of Interpersonal Behavior*. He refined the theory in his 1994 book, *The Human Element: Productivity, Self-Esteem and the Bottom Line*. Where I am not drawing on Schutz, I'm either using the research into social loafing by Max Ringelmann, Alan Ingham et al, Tan & Tan, and Klehe & Anderson (their papers are listed in the bibliography) or relying on my own executive coaching experience (which has highlighted the presence of worldview limiting beliefs).

[43] How the Individual beliefs and values connect with the 16 behaviours (page 196)

- The "I am insignificant" limiting belief often causes these three behaviours – repeatedly avoiding meetings, repeatedly turning up late for meetings and repeatedly not speaking up at meetings. It spawns the fear of being ignored or dismissed, which – if it happened – confirms the belief that you are someone who doesn't matter. So people who repeatedly avoid meetings think they'll sidestep the risk of being ignored by getting their retaliation in first ("I'll ignore you before you ignore me"). People who turn up late repeatedly are using a subtler defence against the risk of being ignored: "I'll show I'm significant and can't be ignored by arriving after you and telling you it's because I'm busy and therefore important." Finally, a pattern of staying silent in meetings is an obvious way to avoid being ignored. After all, if you say nothing, you won't experience yourself being ignored. However, the worldview belief, "I can't trust anybody here" – where people fear being hurt, punished or ostracised if they open up – may also drive a repeated failure to speak up. By the way, note that I said these three behaviours are often caused by the "I am insignificant" belief. Non-belief causes can also be present. One is non-interest in the group's aim. Another is the absence of any compelling group purpose.
- Sullen body language – a form of passive aggression – is often driven by the "I am not good enough" belief. If so, it reflects irritation with the member's low influence over the group's direction or decisions. But the other two self-image limiting beliefs could also drive it, either on their own or working in concert with the "not good enough" belief. For example, if a member feels he's not being included, that no one values his presence, his "I am insignificant" belief may kick in, meaning he doesn't speak up and make himself heard (to avoid being ignored) even though he resents his urge to stay silent, which shows in his body language. Or he may have felt rejected by another member, triggering pain from the "I am unlovable/unlikeable" belief, resulting in resentful silence and sullen body language.

- Social loafing is a complex group problem with many possible causes, only some of which concern members' limiting beliefs and values. Endnote 41 explores social loafing in greater detail. To keep this short, we can say that loafing in groups may be due to a person's low conscientiousness, low organisational citizenship or high individualism (values) or context issues like boring, low-importance tasks. But equally, it could be driven by the "insignificant" or "not good enough" limiting beliefs making it hard for members to include or assert themselves because they're afraid of experiencing their unimportance ("no one will listen") or competence ("I'll only mess things up in public, which will feel humiliating"). A worldview belief that "people in power have special privilege" can also encourage social loafing.

- Hidden agendas can be due to all three self-image limiting beliefs. A lack of self-significance can make someone hide their aims or views for fear of being ignored. A sense that we're not good enough can make us afraid to assert influence in a group for fear of experiencing our powerlessness. And a sense that people don't like us can mean we don't open up about our aims. It's also possible that members may hold worldview limiting beliefs like "I can't trust anybody here", causing them to hide their plans and real opinions while, despite their public silence, they work behind the scenes towards personal aims opposing the group's stated objectives.

- Pairing up and cliques, like hidden agendas, can stem from one or more limiting beliefs. For example, fears about our ability to intervene powerfully and skilfully ("not good enough" belief) or feeling we are the odd one out (a result of the "I'm unlovable" belief). You'll see this behaviour driven by two or more members who feel frustrated or unneeded and want to create an alliance to boost their power or gain emotional support to avoid their fear of rejection.

- The wish to avoid blame and duck responsibility is often behind repeated finger-pointing, a defence mechanism caused by the "not good enough" belief.

- Limiting beliefs aren't the sole drivers of power struggles; they may simply reflect strongly held opposing opinions. However, intellectual differences can become entrenched if accompanied by "I am not good enough" (self-image) or "I don't trust anybody's motives" (worldview) beliefs that turn a preference for one's opinion into a battle for dominance.

- The problem of leaders over-controlling or micromanaging is, in my experience, usually due to their subconscious limiting beliefs about their leadership ability – in other words, the "I am not good enough" belief is affecting them. But their view that others' standards of workmanship won't match their own (a worldview belief) can also drive this behaviour.

- Leaders who under-delegate, crush opponents, block debate or avoid responsibility usually suffer from the "I am not good enough" belief.

- The problem of members not saying what they're thinking and feeling (the "elephant in the room") can have many causes: a dictatorial leader, groupthink or a distrustful atmosphere due to the group's history. But equally, it may flow from all three self-image limiting beliefs combined and, in addition, a worldview that "you can't trust anybody so it's best to limit what you say". The same is true of *executive sabotage*.

- Members not delivering on their promises repeatedly usually indicates low commitment to the group's purpose or unspoken disagreement with a recent decision or a failure to put the shared goal ahead of selfish interests. (Note: this assumes the members in question have the ability to deliver.) But self-image limiting beliefs may also be present. Ask yourself, why don't the non-delivering members speak up and disagree with the goal or decision when they're together? And why do the other members repeatedly fail to challenge them on their non-delivery? It could be due to any of the three self-image limiting beliefs, singly or combined. Members may feel they have no right to challenge the goal, decision or under-delivering member ("not significant enough"). Or they may feel they lack the social skill ("not good enough"). Or they may fear rejection ("not likable") if they voice their true feelings.

Bibliography

Mentioned in the text or endnotes

Bales, Robert. *Interaction Process Analysis; A Method for the Study of Small Groups.* Addison-Wesley Press, Cambridge, Massachusetts, 1950.

Belbin, Meredith. *Management Teams: Why They Succeed or Fail.* Butterworth Heinemann, Oxford, 1981.

Benson, Jarlath. *Working More Creatively with Groups* (second edition). Routledge, 2001

Bion, Wilfried. *Experiences in Groups.* Brunner Routledge, New York, 1961.

Financial Services Authority Board. *The Failure of the Royal Bank of Scotland* report. December 2011.

Garland, J., Jones H. and Kolodny, R. *A Model of Stages in the Development of Social Work Groups.* Published in Explorations in Group Work: Essays in theory and practice (edited by S. Bernstein), Boston University School of Social Work, Boston, 1965.

Geddes, Linda. UK Riots: *Why Respectable People Turned to Looting.* New Scientist, 12 August 2011.

Janis, Irving. Groupthink: *Psychological Studies of Polities Decisions and Fiascoes* (second edition). Wadsworth, Boston, 1982.

Katzenbach, Jon & Smith, Douglas. *The Wisdom of Teams*, HarperCollins, 1993.

Kerr, James. *Legacy.* Constable, London, 2013.

Keyton, Joann. *Group Termination.* Article in Small Group Research, February 1993.

Klehe, Ute-Christine and Anderson, Neil. *The Moderating Influence of Personality and Culture on Social Loafing in Typical Versus Maximum Performance Situations.* International Journal of Selection & Assessment 15(2): 250–262, June 2007.

Lacoursiere, Roy. *The Life Cycle of Groups: Group Development Stage Theory.* Kluwer Academic / Plenum Publishers, 1980.

Le Bon, Gustave. The Crowd: A Study of the Popular Mind (1895).

Lewin, Kurt. Resolving Social Conflicts. Harper & Row, 1948.

Lewis, Paul et al. Reading The Riots: Investigating England's Summer of Disorder. Report by The Guardian and London School of Economics & Political Science, December 2011.

Myers, David. *Psychology.* (International edition). Worth Publishers, New York, 2013.

Myers, David and Bishop, George. *Discussion effects on racial attitudes.* Science, 21 August 1970, pp. 778–779.

Parisi-Carew, Eunice. *Why Teams Fail – and What to Do About It.* Article in Human Resource Executive Online. Publication date unknown.

Ringelmann, Max. *Appareils De Cultur Mecanique avec Treuils et Cables (Resultats D'essais).* Article in Annales de l'Institut National Agronomique, 1913.

Rioch, Margaret. *The Work of Wilfred Bion on Groups.* Article in the Journal for the Study of Interpersonal Processes (1970, Vol 33, Issue 1, pp 56–66).

Schutz, William. *Profound Simplicity: Foundations for a Social Philosophy.* Bantam Books, 1979.

Schutz, William. *The Human Element, The Human Element: Productivity, Self-Esteem and the Bottom Line.* Jossey-Bass, 1994.

Schutz William. *FIRO: A Three-Dimensional Theory of Interpersonal Behavior.* Rhinehart, New York, 1958.

Simms, Ashley and Nichols, Tommy. *Social Loafing: A Review of the Literature.* Journal of Management Policy and Practice 15(1), January 2014.

Tabrizi, Behnam. *75% of Cross Functional Teams Are Dysfunctional.* Harvard Business Review, 23 June 2015.

Tajfel, Henri and Turner, J. *The Social Identity Theory of Intergroup Behaviour.* A chapter in Psychology of Intergroup Relations, 1986 1986, 7–24.

Tan, H.W. & Tan, L.T. *Organizational Citizenship Behavior and Social Loafing: The Role of Personality, Motives and Contextual Factors.* Article in the Journal of Psychology 142(1): 89–108, February 2008.

Topping, Alexandra and Diski, Rebekah and Clifton, Helen. *The Women Who Rioted.* Article in The Guardian, 9 December 2011

Tuckman, Bruce. *Developmental Sequence in Small Groups.* Article in Psychological Bulletin, 1965 (vol. 63, pp. 384–399).

Twomey, Liam. *England's Euro 2016 failure a result of "culture of fear" – Steven Gerrard.* Published on ESPN website, 30 June 2016. http://www.espnfc.com/england/story/2904324/englands-euro-2016-failure-a-result-of-culture-of-fear-steven-gerrard

Wageman, Ruth et al. *Senior Leadership Teams.* Harvard Business School Press, Boston, 2008.

Other

Belbin, Meredith. *Team Roles at Work.* Routledge, London, 1993.

Belbin, Meredith. *Changing the Way We Work.* Butterworth Heinemann, Oxford, 1999.

Clutterbuck, David. *Coaching the Team at Work.* Nicolas Brealey International, London, 2007.

Eastwood, Owen. *Belonging: the Ancient Code of Togetherness.* Quercus, London, 2021.

Forsyth, Donelson. *Group Dynamics* (third edition). Wadsworth, Belmont, 1999.

Gilson, Clive et al. *Peak Performance.* Profile Books, London, 2003.

Hawkins, Peter. *Leadership Team Coaching.* Kogan Page, London, 2011.

Hayes, Phil. *Leading and Coaching Teams to Success.* Open University Press, Maidenhead, 2011.

Jansen, Jeff. *Championship Team Building.* Winning the Mental Game, Carey, 1999.

Katzenbach, Jon. *Teams at the Top.* Harvard Business School Press, Boston, 1998.

Katzenbach, Jon and Smith, Douglas. *The Discipline of Teams.* John Wiley & Sons & Sons, New York, 2001.

Larson, Carl and LaFasto, Frank. *Teamwork: What Must Go Right/What Can Go Wrong.* Sage Publications, London, 1989.

Leary-Joyce, John and Lines, Hilary. *Systemic Team Coaching.* AoEC Press, St Albans, 2018.

Leigh, Andrew and Maynard, Michael. *Leading Your Team.* Nicolas Brealey Publishing, London, 2002.

Lencioni, Patrick. *Overcoming the Five Dysfunctions of a Team: a Field Guide.* Jossey-Bass, San Francisco, 2005.

Levi, Daniel. *Group Dynamics for Teams.* Sage Publications, London, 2001.

Macmillan, Pat. *The Performance Factor: Unlocking the Secrets of Teamwork.* B & H Publishing, Tennessee, 2001.

Margerison, Charles and McCann, Dick. *Team Management: Practical New Approaches.* Management Books 2000, Chalford, 1990.

Robbins, Harvey and Finley, Michael. *Why Teams Don't Work.* Orion Business Books, London, 1996.

Scouller, James. *The Three Levels of Leadership: How to Develop Your Leadership Presence, Knowhow and Skill* (second edition). Management Books 2000, Oxford, 2016.

Shaw, Marvin. *Group Dynamics: the Psychology of Small Group Behavior.* McGraw-Hill, New York, 1976.

Syer, John and Connolly, Christopher. *How Teamwork Works.* McGraw-Hill, London, 1996.

Thornton, Christine. *Group and Team Coaching.* Routledge, Hove, 2010.

Walker, Sam. *The Captain Class.* Ebury Press, London, 2017.

Whitaker, David. *The Spirit of Teams.* The Crowood Press, 1999.

Widdowson, Lucy and Barber, Paul. *Building Top Performing Teams.* Kogan Page London, 2021.

Woodward, Clive. *Winning!* Hodder & Stoughton, 2004.

Index

A
avoidance 38, 186

B
Bales, Robert 209
Bay of Pigs 39, 188
before-and-after team profiles 17
Belbin team roles 121–123
Belbin, Meredith 121, 155, 208, 209
beliefs 32, 33, 34, 40, 41–43, 189–193
Benson, Jarlath 205, 209
Bion, Wilfred 175–176, 209, 213

C
Chelsea football club 186
collective forces 33–40, 177–188
    avoidance 38, 186
    effects on work teams 38, 185
    focus on external enemies 39, 187
    groupthink 38, 186, 188
    leader dependency 38, 185
    leader scapegoating 38, 186
    story force 35, 179
    survival force 37, 184
    teams as living systems 33–34, 37, 177–188
Combine
    individual members' focus 139
    members' behavioural preferences 143
    members' early questions 138
    members' typical behaviour 141
    problems to watch out for 146
    quick introduction 100
    relationships and roles 140
    resolution of issue 147
    self-esteem complications 144
    team composition 138
    team purpose and goals 138

Combust
    individual members' focus 132
    members' behavioural preferences 133
    members' early questions 131
    members' typical behaviour 132
    problems to watch out for 135
    quick introduction 99
    relationships and roles 132
    resolution of issue 136
    self-esteem complications 133
    team composition 130
    team purpose and goals 130
Commit
    individual members' focus 124
    members' behavioural preferences 125
    members' early questions 123
    members' typical behaviour 125
    problems to watch out for 128
    quick introduction 98
    relationships and roles 125
    resolution of issue 129
    self-esteem complications 127
    team composition 121
    team purpose and goal 120
Commit-Combust-Combine model
    conditions to be met 110–113
    explanation (big picture) 95–118
    explanation (detailed) 119–160
    how long does it take? 110
    infinity loop diagram 95
    issues not phases 103
    micro issues 105
        different speeds 107
        implications 109
        shift moments 106
    overview table (full) 149–151
    overview table (simplistic) 102

three differences versus FIRO theory 208

tools 151–153

upward spiral diagram 109

why the sequence 103

D

Deci, Edward 205

defensive behaviours 107, 126, 127–128, 133–135, 144–146, 192–193, 196, 200, 213

definition 204, 213

three conditions 204

Dual Forces model

description (longer) 175–196

description (shorter) 31–33

diagram 32, 175

E

emotional combustion chamber 45, 196

endings (limited-lifespan teams) 165–167

England football team 36, 182–183, 187, 211–112

Estenson, Professor Jerry 63, 206

extrinsic motivation 205

F

Ferguson, Sir Alex 14

FIFA 37, 184

FIRO theory 96, 207

focus on external enemies 39, 187

Form-Storm-Norm-Perform 96

Frankenstein's monster 37, 185

G

Geddes, Linda 209–210

Grant, Adam 205

groupthink 38, 186, 188

Bay of Pigs 188

Royal Bank of Scotland 188

Guardiola, Pep 14

guilt 193

H

Handforth parish council 23

hidden psychology of teams and groups 29–47, 173–198

high-performance team 54, 60–64

dark side 62

different to high performing team 62

emerges (not built) 55

rarity 60

three distinguishing features 61

I

indefinite-lifespan teams

long-term evolution 162

twelve downward curve scenarios 163–164

individual forces 40–45, 189–196

effects on work teams 44, 195

limiting values 43, 193–194

self-image limiting beliefs 42, 192

worldview limiting beliefs 41, 191

intrinsic motivation 205

section in The Three Levels of Leadership 206

J

Janis, Irving 176, 188, 209, 213

joint accountability 30, 74, 80, 86, 91, 101, 112, 118, 142, 143, 145, 147–148, 158, 166, 174, 208

silent peer pressure 143

two facets 137

K

Katzenbach & Smith 52, 58, 60, 72, 84, 205, 206

Killian, Lewis 211

L

Lacoursiere, Roy 209

leader dependency 38, 185

leader scapegoating 186

leadership
    shared 54, 62, 73, 80, 85, 143, 149,
        159
Le Bon, Gustave 176, 209, 210, 213
Leicester City football club 60
Lewin, Kurt 209
limited-lifespan teams 161
    endings 165
limiting beliefs 42
    self-image 192
    values 43, 193
    worldview 41, 191
living systems 33–34, 37, 39, 177–178,
    185, 188, 199
    formation 178
    survival drive 37, 184

M
Martin Murphy (SAS soldier) 62
micro issues 105–110
    implications 109–110
Mormon Church 181
motivation 88
    extrinsic 205
    intrinsic 205
Myers, David 209

N
New Zealand All Blacks 184, 200, 212

P
performance group 53
    definition 53
    different challenges versus real team
        69–70
    different disciplines versus real team
        70–72
    disadvantages 76
    not a one-time choice 77
    senior 84–86
    when it's a better choice 75–76
potential team 55
    stuckness – five causes 57–59

pseudo team 55
    examples 56–57
psychology of teams and groups (hidden)
    29–47, 173–198

R
real team 54
    advantages 76
    as a living system 177
    definition 54
    different challenges versus
        performance group 69–70
    different disciplines versus
        performance group 70–71
    endings 165–167
    examples 54
    examples of collective outputs 75
    joint accountability. See joint
        accountability
    life cycles diagram 162
    long-term evolution 162
    not a one-time choice 77
    senior 84–86
    twelve downward curve scenarios
        163–164
    why it takes effort to create 29
Ringelmann, Max 205, 209, 214
    social loafing experiment 214
rocket science 13
Roman Catholic church 37, 184
Rubik's Cube 13
Ryan, Richard 205

S
sabotage 196
Schutz, William 96, 166, 176, 204, 205,
    207–208, 209, 215
    fitting a wheel analogy 106
    on psychology of endings 166
self-esteem 190, 200
self-image beliefs 190
senior performance group
    differences versus senior real team 85–86

senior team
  differences versus senior performance group 85–86
  five blocks 89
  rarity 84
shame 192–193
shared leadership 54, 62, 73, 80, 85, 143, 149, 159
social loafing 43, 194, 214
Special Air Services (SAS) 62
  shared leadership 62
story force 35–37
  equation 34, 179
  examples of effects 36–37, 181–184
survival force 37–39, 184
  examples of effects 38
system (living) 33–34, 37, 39, 177–178, 185, 188, 189
system (team as a) 34, 178

T
Tabrizi, Behnam 14
Tajfel, Henri 210, 213
task group 53
  six basic disciplines 70–72
TeamFixer® tool 22, 95, 104, 109, 165
team leader
  can block team formation 76
  contributes creative work 73, 85
  over-dependence on 38, 48, 185
  scapegoating 38, 48, 186
  sharing leadership responsibility 61–62
  when he or she changes 164
Team Progression Curve 52–57
  metaphor for 57
teams
  hidden psychology 29–47, 173–198
  indefinite-lifespan 161
  limited-lifespan 161, 166
teamwork (not *the* key to teams) 59–60
Thatcher, Margaret 185, 186
The Three Levels of Leadership 7, 8, 9, 121, 193

The Wisdom of Teams 53
Tuckman, Bruce 96, 103, 132, 165, 207, 209
Turner, Ralph 211
Twomey, Liam 211

V
values 190

W
Whitaker, David 205
worldview limiting beliefs 41, 191

About the Author

James Scouller is an executive coach, thought leader and author. His fascination with leadership has dominated his working life over the last 45 years. It's been the golden thread connecting his four books.

What sets his work apart? His focus on the previously ignored psychological challenges facing leaders and their teams.

His first book, *The Three Levels of Leadership*, came out in 2011 with a second edition in 2016. You could call it a self-help manual for leaders. It offered them new models and tools for growing their presence, knowhow and skill under pressure.

He released his trilogy, *How to Build Winning Teams Again and Again*, in 2024. James sees this as a companion series to "Three Levels".

After living and working in different countries, he led three international companies as CEO for 11 years before founding his executive coaching practice, The Scouller Partnership, in 2004. Today, when he's not writing, he coaches leaders and their teams. He has two postgraduate coaching qualifications and trained in applied psychology for four years at the UK Institute of Psychosynthesis. He also holds a 4th Dan black belt in Aikido, a Japanese martial art. He lives near London with his wife, Tricia, and their dog, Matilda.

If you'd like to get in touch with him, download his free tools, watch his videos or read his articles on leadership and teams, you can visit his website at **www.leadershipmasterysuite.com.**